**Cultural And
Geographical
Exploration**

# Mysteries
of the Sahara

### CHRONICLES FROM *NATIONAL GEOGRAPHIC*

## Cultural And Geographical Exploration

**Cultural And
Geographical
Exploration**

# Mysteries
# of the Sahara

## CHRONICLES FROM *NATIONAL GEOGRAPHIC*

Arthur M. Schlesinger, jr.
*Senior Consulting Editor*

Fred L. Israel
*General Editor*

CHELSEA HOUSE PUBLISHERS

*Philadelphia*

**CHELSEA HOUSE PUBLISHERS**

*Editor in Chief* Stephen Reginald
*Managing Editor* James D. Gallagher
*Production Manager* Pamela Loos
*Art Director* Sara Davis
*Director of Photography* Judy L. Hasday
*Senior Production Editor* Lisa Chippendale

First Printing

1 3 5 7 9 8 6 4 2

**Library of Congress Cataloging-in-Publication Data**

Mysteries of the Sahara: chronicles from National Geographic /
Arthur M. Schlesinger, jr., Fred L. Israel.
    p.   cm.—(Cultural and geographical exploration)
    Includes bibliographical references and index.
    ISBN 0-7910-5097-1
    1. Africa, North— Description and travel.   I. Schlesinger, Arthur
  Meier, 1917–    . II. Israel, Fred L.   III. Series.
  DT165.2.M97 1998
  961—dc21                         98-36695
                                            CIP

# CONTENTS

# "THE GREATEST EDUCATIONAL JOURNAL"

When the first *National Geographic* magazine appeared in October 1888, the United States totaled 38 states. Grover Cleveland was President. The nation's population hovered around 60 million. Great Britain's Queen Victoria also ruled as the Empress of India. William II became Kaiser of Germany that year. Tsar Alexander III ruled Russia and the Turkish Empire stretched from the Balkans to the tip of Arabia. To Westerners, the Far East was still a remote and mysterious land. Throughout the world, riding the back of an animal was the principle means of transportation. Unexplored and unmarked places dotted the global map.

On January 13, 1888, thirty-three men—scientists, cartographers, inventors, scholars, and explorers—met in Washington, D. C. They had accepted an invitation from Gardiner Greene Hubbard (1822-1897), the first president of the Bell Telephone Co. and a leader in the education of the deaf, to form the National Geographic Society "to increase and diffuse geographic knowledge." One of the assembled group noted that they were the "first explorers of the Grand Canyon and the Yellowstone, those who had carried the American flag farthest north, who had measured the altitude of our famous mountains, traced the windings of our coasts and rivers, determined the distribution of flora and fauna, enlightened us in the customs of the aborigines, and marked out the path of storm and flood." Nine months later, the first issue of *National Geographic* magazine was sent out to 165 charter members. Today, more than a century later, membership has grown to an astounding 11 million in more than 170 nations. Several times that number regularly read the monthly issues of the *National Geographic* magazine.

The first years were difficult ones for the new magazine. The earliest volumes seem dreadfully scientific and quite dull. The articles in Volume I, No. 1 set the tone—W. M Davis, "Geographic Methods in Geologic Investigation," followed by W. J. McGee, "The Classification of Geographic Forms by Genesis." Issues came out erratically—three in 1889, five in 1890, four in 1891; and two in 1895. In January 1896 "an illustrated monthly" was added to the title. The November issue that year contained a photograph of a half-naked Zulu bride and bridegroom in their wedding finery staring full face into the camera. But, a reader must have wondered what to make of the accompanying text: "These people . . . possess some excellent traits, but are horribly cruel when once they have smelled blood." In hopes of expanding circulation, the Board of Managers offered newsstand copies at $.25 each and began to accept advertising. But the magazine essentially remained unchanged. Circulation only rose slightly.

In January 1898, shortly after Gardiner Greene Hubbard's death, his son-in-law Alexander Graham Bell (1847-1922) agreed to succeed him as the second president of the National Geographic Society. Bell invented the telephone in 1876 and, while pursuing his life long goal of improving the lot of the deaf, had turned his amazingly versatile mind to contemplating such varied problems as human flight, air conditioning, and popularizing geography. The society then had about 1100 members—the magazine was on the edge of bankruptcy. Bell did not want the job. He wrote in his diary though that he accepted leadership of the Society "in order to save it. Geography is a fascinating subject and it can be made interesting," he told the board of directors. Bell abandoned the unsuccessful attempt to increase circulation through newsstand sales. "Our journal," he wrote "should go to members, people who believe in our work and want to help." He understood that the lure for prospective members should be an association with a society that made it possible for the average person to share with kings and scientists the excitement of sending an expedition to a strange land or an explorer to an inaccessible region. This idea, more than any other, has been responsible for the growth of the National Geographic Society and for the popularity of the magazine. "I can well remember," recalled Bell in 1912, "how the idea was laughed at that we should ever reach a membership of ten thousand." That year it had soared to 107,000!

Bell attributed this phenomenal growth though to one man who had transformed the *National Geographic* magazine into "the greatest educational journal in the world"—Gilbert H. Grosvenor (1875-1966). Bell had hired the then 24-year-old Grosvenor in 1899 as the Society's first full-time employee "to put some life into the magazine." He personally escorted the new editor, who will become his son-in-law, to the Society's headquarters—a small rented room shared with the American Forestry Association on the fifth floor of a building, long since gone, across 15th street from the U. S. Treasury in downtown Washington. Grosvenor remembered the headquarters "littered with old magazines, newspapers, and a few record books and six enormous boxes crammed with *Geographics* returned by the newsstands." "No desk!" exclaimed Bell. "I'll send you mine." That afternoon, delivery men brought Grosvenor a large walnut rolltop and the new editor began to implement Bell's instructions—to transform the magazine from one of cold geographic fact "expressed in hieroglyphic terms which the layman could not understand into a vehicle for carrying the living, breathing, human-interest truth about this great world of ours to the people." And what did Bell consider appropriate "geographic subjects?" He replied: "The world and all that is in it is our theme."

Grosvenor shared Bell's vision of a great society and magazine which would disseminate geographic knowledge. "I thought of geography in terms of its Greek root: *geographia*—a description of the world," he later wrote. "It thus becomes the most catholic of subjects, universal in appeal, and embracing nations, people, plants, birds, fish. We would never lack interesting subjects." To attract readers, Grosvenor had to change the public attitude toward geography which he knew was regarded as "one of the dullest of all subjects, something to inflict upon schoolboys and avoid in later life." He wondered why certain books which relied heavily on geographic description remained popular—Charles Darwin's *Voyage of the Beagle*, Richard Dana, Jr.'s *Two Years Before the Mast* and even Herodotus' *History*. Why did readers for generations, and with Herodotus' travels, for twenty centuries return to these books? What did these volumes, which used so many geographic descriptions, have in common? What was the secret? According to Grosvenor, the answer was that "each was an accurate, eyewitness, firsthand account. Each contained simple straightforward writing—writing that sought to make pictures in the reader's mind."

Gilbert Grosvenor was editor of the *National Geographic* magazine for 55 years, from 1899 until 1954. Each of the 660 issues under his direction had been a highly readable geography textbook. He took Bell's vision and made it a reality. Acclaimed as "Mr. Geography," he discovered the earth anew for himself and for millions around the globe. He charted the dynamic course which the National Geographic Society and its magazine followed for more than half a century. In so doing, he forged an instrument for world education and understanding unique in this or any age. Under his direction, the *National Geographic* magazine grew from a few hundred copies—he recalled carrying them to the post office on his back—to more than five million at the time of his retirement as editor, enough for a stack 25 miles high.

This Chelsea House series celebrates Grosvenor's first twenty-five years as editor of the *National Geographic*. "The mind must see before it can believe," said Grosvenor. From the earliest days, he filled the magazine with photographs and established another Geographic principle—to portray people in their natural attire or lack of it. Within his own editorial committee, young Grosvenor encountered the prejudice that photographs had to be "scientific." Too often, this meant dullness. To Grosvenor, every picture and sentence had to be interesting to the layman. "How could you educate and inform if you lost your audience by boring your readers?" Grosvenor would ask his staff. He persisted and succeeded in making the *National Geographic* magazine reflect this fascinating world.

To the young-in-heart of every age there is magic in the name *National Geographic*. The very words conjure up enchanting images of faraway places, explorers and scientists, sparkling seas and dazzling mountain peaks, strange plants, animals, people, and customs. The small society founded in 1888 "for the increase and diffusion of geographic knowledge" grew, under the guidance of one man, to become a great force for knowledge and understanding. This achievement lies in the genius of Gilbert H. Grosvenor, the architect and master builder of the National Geographic Society and its magazine.

Fred L. Israel
*The City College of the City University of New York*

# MYSTERIES OF THE SAHARA: AN OVERVIEW

## Fred L. Israel

The nations we know as Morocco, Algeria, Tunisia, and Libya occupy most of an area which medieval Arab geographers called the Maghreb, "the land where the sun sets in front of the ocean." This region has three distinctive geographical features which separate it from the rest of the African continent—the Sahara desert, the Atlas mountain chain stretching from west to east; and the Mediterranean Sea in the north. More than 300 miles of desert separate the western part of Libya from Egypt. Therefore, this land island was virtually isolated from the Nile valley except for a coastal caravan route. The Maghreb resembles Chile in shape but it stretches east and west instead of north and south. Access for invaders from any direction except the Mediterranean was barred by formidable mountains filled with steep valleys and narrow gorges which change gradually into desert, in parts stony and in others sand with oases of palm trees. However, there are not many natural barriers between the four nations of this region.

The Maghreb has few rivers which could be used for irrigation. Therefore, the volume and the time of rainfall has determined human settlements. The coastal plain along the Mediterranean is the most fertile land. Here olive and cork trees flourish. Grain is cultivated. Scrub brush provides a land cover just south of the plain not unlike that of Spain, southern France, or parts of California. Here, the principle crops include figs, almonds, olives, and grapes. In the desert regions, the date is the staple crop—and the only part of the Maghreb where camels were raised. But throughout the entire area, rainfall is irregular and disastrous in its unpredictability. Hot sand storms often blow off from the Sahara and parch the earth. Historically, human beings and their animals have deforested this area resulting in the erosion of scarce topsoil.

Ports on the Mediterranean linked the Maghreb with the Iberian peninsula, Italy, and Egypt. The main trading routes which joined the Mahgreb with the rest of Africa ran north to south—through the settled areas and then a chain of oases to the southern fringe of the Sahara and beyond. There routes came to the sea through stretches of cultivated land. It is at these points that cities grew up. Two such areas were of particular importance during the 19th and early part of the 20th century. One lay on the Atlantic coast of Morocco and the cities of Fez and Marrakish. The other was along the central plain of Tunisia where Tunis, near the site of the ancient city of Carthage, became important in trade as well as one of the leading spiritual and intellectual centers of the Islamic world. These two areas radiated their economic, political, and spiritual power over the land around and between them.

Over the past 3000 years, many peoples have passed through the Maghreb—Phonicians; Romans; Vandals; Byzantines; Turks; Spaniards; the French, and most important of all, the Arabs. The last came in two great waves, mainly in the seventh and eighth and then in the eleventh and twelfth centuries. The word "Arab" is ambiguous. That is because Islam does not recognize distinction of nations or races as being important. Islam forms an all-embracing community for its adherents. Since the overwhelming majority of Arabs are Muslim, the Western concept of nationality has had to compete with the religious concept of Islam as the locus for group feeling. The consequence is that Islam contains many ethnic types which permeate the Maghreb area, types ethnically distinct only to the mind of a Westerner preoccupied with differences of race and nationality. For example, the indigenous peoples of North Africa, the Berbers, who still live as nomads in goat-hair tents or as sedentary farmers in stone houses, consider themselves Muslims.

"Here and There in Northern Africa" is a fascinating account of the Maghreb just prior to the First World War (1914-18). It is an excellent description of the varied peoples—and their customs—who lived here. The 113 illustrations make this a unique record of an area which is still considered by Westerners as being remote and mysterious.

# HERE AND THERE
# IN NORTHERN AFRICA

### By Frank Edward Johnson

*Author of "The Mole Men: An Account of the Troglodytes of Southern Tunisia" (October, 1911), "The Sacred City of the Sands" (December, 1911), and "The Greek Bronzes of Tunisia" (January, 1912), etc., in the* National Geographic Magazine.

### I
### THE MOUNTAIN-CLIMBING TROGLODYTES OF TUNISIA

SIDI HADJ, the Holy Man, or *Marabout,* and his five sons were most hospitable people, and we had gotten to know each other well during my stay at the Cadhi's. There was seldom an evening when the venerable old "pilgrim," with his long, white, flowing beard and his green turban, did not drop in to have dinner with the Cadhi.

Our table could only seat eight, and it was always full; sometimes a sheik from the hinterland of Tripoli or a Touareg chief who had come for provisions. Many had never sat in a chair at a table before or had seen knives, forks, and spoons in use. They would watch the Cadhi and copy him.

With them a great platter of native wheat is brought in with a half or a whole sheep or lamb. The eldest son of the hosts cuts it into long strips; it is then pulled to pieces with the fingers, and each one takes from the huge dish the portion directly in front of him. Any dainty morsel is carefully put in front of the guest of honor. One or two bowls, or loving cups, are filled with water and passed around when one is thirsty.

Arabs eat to live, not live to eat, and, as a rule, they do not indulge in overeating. An ordinary Arab can live on a few handfuls of barley and some dried dates, water, and a cup of coffee. A European would die if forced to live on the same diet.

### CAVE-DWELLERS OF THE MOUNTAINS

All the Troglodyte strongholds are wild and difficult of approach; hence lay their security in

1

THE WALLS OF SOUSSE, TUNISIA                    Photo by Neurdein

This ancient city was an important town when Carthage was in all its glory and it was spared by the Romans when they destroyed Carthage in 146 B. C. Like all Arab coast towns, it is protected by a wall.

time of war. Their warriors could see the enemy approaching for many miles, unless they came by night, and then the zigzag path that led up to the great walls was too dangerous, for a stumble meant sudden death on the rocks hundreds of feet below.

Guermessa, the ancestral home of Sidi Hadj and his five sons, is one of the wildest and most difficult Troglodyte towns to reach. It is situated on the top of a sugar-loaf mountain, the sides of which rise precipitously for hundreds of feet (see page 5). The narrow zigzag trail has been worn smooth by centuries of hard use, and the surface of the rock is like polished marble. It is even difficult for the mountain goats, born and bred at Guermessa; therefore, how much more difficult for man and beast!

The inhabitants of Guermessa are a fierce, warlike race, who look with suspicion upon Troglodytes of other districts and with hatred on a stranger. Many were the looks of hatred cast at me by the inhabitants of the rock caves as we wound around the narrow and slippery trail in front of their dwellings.

My companions, Mohammed and Brebisch, were very quiet; this was unknown country to them, and they remembered the stories told in their childhood about their great enemy, the Troglodyte town of Guermessa.

A CARAVAN ON THE MARCH

Photo by Bougalt

Here we see an Arab family on a journey. How carefully the privacy of the women is secured, even under the difficulties of travel, is shown by the fully draped palanquin for their use on the camel in the center of the picture.

About three months in the year the inhabitants of Guermessa live in their stone caves, dug deep into the sides of the mountain. Nine months of the year they spend as nomads on the borders of the Great Sahara, or in their *gourbis*—tents made of goats' and camels' hair woven together—on the mountain side, where their great herds of long-haired goats, broad-tailed sheep, and young camels can find pasturage.

Down in the valleys are to be found plantations of superb olive and fig trees, and here and there fields of barley. Every drop of rain has filtered down to the valley, and by a system of crude but practical stone walls the fields have been terraced, one below the other, so that all the water has been utilized; not one drop goes to waste.

When the olives and figs begin to ripen, the Troglodytes leave a few trustworthy men in their *ksar*, or fortified storehouse and citadel, fully armed, of course, and the rest move down to the valleys, where they can protect their olive and fig groves, for unless the fields were guarded day and night all the olives and figs would be stolen by Troglodytes of other districts.

Unlike the underground cave-dwellers of Matmata and the Houaia Mountains, the men of Guermessa have separate establishments for themselves, their wives and families.

How many caves were owned in Guermessa by the sons and grandsons of Sidi Hadj is impossible for me to state, but they owned a great number.

THE INTERIOR OF A CAVE-DWELLING

Sidi Hadj's own cave was large, and the rear part of the floor was raised about a foot higher than the front of the cave. Rugs from Kairowan and Persia were laid over the stone floor and numerous Touareg leather cushions stuffed with sheeps' wool were strewn about.

These thick Oriental rugs were intended to sleep on and not to walk upon. The uneven stone floor of a Troglodyte cave is a very un-

A NATIVE MOUNTED POLICEMAN OF THE SAHARA

This man belongs to the mounted police force, called the *oudjac*, which is commanded partly by French and partly by native officers. This force patrols the country, and one is as safe in Algeria and Tunisia as in any occidental land. Note the curious straw hat, with its brim some four feet in diameter.

comfortable place to sleep on, but use a couple of thick Oriental rugs and cover oneself with a *bernous*, or Arab cloak, and you have a most comfortable bed.

On the stone walls of the cave hung a miniature arsenal of flint-lock pistols and long-barreled guns and shotguns. A very large wooden chest, painted green, with Moorish designs in red and gold, stood at the back of the cave, which was about 7 feet high by 14 feet wide and about 24 feet deep.

Two Persian pictures of Mecca decorated the walls, and some ornamental *bernous* for wearing during a fantasia (see page 9), and the usual *cous-cous* plates and platters brought from Ghadames, usually used for decoration by the Troglodytes. They reminded me of our Indian woven plates and baskets of certain tribes of the Far West and New Mexico. They are so well woven that they hold water or liquid like a dish, and they have simple but decorative patterns worked in color.

Being far away from the wells, none of our animals were watered that evening. Arab horses of southern Tunisia are watered but once every 24 hours, and frequently not for 48 hours. It seemed to me terribly cruel, but the animals are used to it.

About 5 p. m. is the usual time for watering the horses. Strange to say, when watered they do not seem to want to drink more than half as much as horses in America. They like to splash their noses and heads and play with the water.

We had an excellent dinner, prepared by the wives of Sidi Hadj's sons and Ben Saada, our own remarkable cook. About twelve of us ate first, including Mohammed ben Cadhi and Brebisch ben Kaliphe, my devoted friends and companions during my trip.

Sidi Hadji as host was most picturesque, and he entertained us with wonderful stories of his pilgrimage to Mecca and what he had seen and heard. He described the Kaaba, "The

THE CURIOUS TROGLODYTE TOWN OF GUERMESSA

The inhabitants of this strange town, which is composed of three separate villages, are a fierce, warlike people, as are all the mountain-climbing Troglodytes, or cave-dwellers, of southern Tunisia. Note the odd-shaped houses.

Photo by Soler

TROGLODYTE COURTYARD OR PATIO OF THE SHEIK OF MATMATA,
SHOWING ENTRANCES INTO VARIOUS CAVES

The holes vary in depth and width, but average nine meters deep by fifteen meters in circumference. This great hole is used as a "patio," or courtyard. Numerous caves dug in the sides of the hole serve as living-rooms and storehouses. One enters these dwellings by means of a passage tunneled through the earth or rock. Some of the ceilings are roughly ornamented with Arabic designs cut in bas-relief in the rock and the dates when the dwellings were dug. None of them seem to go back more than 100 years (see text, pages 31, 46).

A LITTLE BEDOUIN GIRL

The girls of this race of desert wanderers are quite attractive, but, owing to the hard life they lead, they soon become old and wrinkled. The women do practically all the labor of the camp—fetching wood, drawing water, pitching and striking the tents, milking the goats and camels, and preparing the food.

THE MORNING PRAYER

The pious Moslem, far out in the desert, with his face turned to the East, in the direction of Mecca, performs the first of those five acts of devotion which punctuate the day of an orthodox son of the Prophet (see page 102).

Photo by Lehnert and Landrock

HORSEMEN READY FOR A FANTASIA

The Arabs greatly delight in these fantasias, which consist of some of the most remarkable feats of horsemanship. The participants dash forward at full speed, twirling their guns about their bodies and over their heads, shouting and firing their guns into the air, when suddenly, at a given signal, the whole line will bring their horses to so abrupt a stop that any but the most accomplished horseman would be immediately unseated.

Holy of Holies,'' that curious rectangular building that contains the great uncut ruby that has turned black on account of the sins of the world and is now known as the Black Stone. He told us that Mecca was a sacred city centuries before Mohammed was born, and the Kaaba was already a great shrine. This is the reason:

## HOW MECCA BECAME A HOLY PLACE

When Abraham led Hagar and her infant son, Ishmael, into the desert and abandoned them to die of hunger and thirst, Ishmael cried for water, and Hagar put him down in the sand and started off in search of water.

The desert lay between two ranges of sand-dunes, or mountains, and Hagar in her anguish crossed this valley seven times, but found no water. Almost exhausted, she dragged herself back to the small child.

Imagine her surprise and joy to see him creeping toward a pool of water that had miraculously sprung up since she had laid him on the sand! The pool was deep, and, fearing the child would fall in and be drowned, she cried out in Arabic: *Zem! Zem!* which, interpreted, means "Stay where you are! Stay where you are!" or "Stop!" And the pool, or well, is known to this day as *Zem-Zem.* Around this spot was built the famous shrine of Mecca, toward which 220 million Mohammedans turn their faces and bow in prayer five times a day at the shrill sound of the muezzin's call to prayer:

"La il-ah-il-ah Allah.
Mohammed ar-ra-sou-la Allah!
Allah is Allah! There is no God but Allah.
Mohammed is the Prophet of God."

As these words rang out that evening at Guermessa my host, his sons, our escort, and the guests left the caves and walked a few steps to where an unbroken view could be had on all sides, and, turning toward Mecca, they knelt and bowed together, touching their foreheads to the ground several times.

None of the Troglodytes ever used a prayer rug; possibly they did in the mosques, but at prayer times I never intruded on their devotions, but out on the mountain sides and on the plains and the Sahara no prayer rug was ever used.

### THE DESERT AT EVENING

The impression of that evening will remain with me as long as memory lasts. Range after range of purple-colored table-land mountains that we had ridden over day by day, hour after hour, loomed up in the distance.

In the foreground the figures of Sidi Hadj, his sons, and the Troglodytes silhouetted against a sunset sky of green and gold; beneath us to the south and west stretched a reddish golden mass of sand—the Great Sahara in all its fascinating mystery.

WILL HE COME?

One of the great attractions of these daughters of the desert is the exquisite grace of their carriage and the unconsciously beautiful poses they adopt when at rest.

Photo by Lehnert and Landrock

A YOUNG GIRL OF EXTREME SOUTHERN TUNISIA

She wears two kinds of ear-rings, with great hoops of solid silver, and a chain of loops dangles down almost as far as her chin, and a charm attached—the hands of Fatima. These hands of Fatima are supposed to bring extraordinary luck. No Arab child or woman is ever without them. Fastening her garment is a curious pin, the kind used all over northern Africa. On her arms are silver open-work bracelets, and dangling from the pin is a silver chain with hands of Fatima and other charms. In countries where poverty is so great that it is impossible to wear these ornaments of silver they are made of a white metal and always greatly decorated.

Almost 2,000 feet below us wound and wriggled what looked like an earthworm—a belated caravan of camels heading toward some *gourbis* (Bedouin tents) whose camp-fire dotted the distant landscape. Everything was still and no one spoke; all felt the spell of that glorious sunset. Even the horses, mules, donkeys, camels, and those vicious, yapping Kabyle dogs seemed quiet.

Twilight lasts about three minutes; then comes utter darkness, when the Troglodytes barricade their gates and doors and unloose their numerous dogs. The day's work was fin-

ished and we had had a hard day's ride. Those thick Persian rugs seemed very tempting.

What mattered it if 18 others slept in the same cave. But I could not let them close and lock the great cave door. A Troglodyte cave has air-tight walls, roof, and floor cut out of solid rock. Sidi Hadj begged and pleaded, saying that we would all be murdered; but I remained firm, and the door remained open.

Undressing is quite simple for an Arab. He takes off some of his garments, unfastens his belt, puts his slippers near him, also his gun or pistol, and rolls himself in his *bernous*. They sleep very heavily, and it is difficult to awaken them.

About 2 a. m. I was awakened by a queer noise that I thought was made by thieves. I grabbed my Browning and waited. All the men in the cave slept soundly. A moonbeam fell through the open door, and I saw a large Kabyle dog creeping into our cave. I threw one of my heavy boots at him and he rushed out howling; but, in spite of the noise, no one stirred. Twenty minutes later back he came; this time my other boot caught him on the head, and he made a fearful noise, but every one slept on.

Photo by Frechon

The fate of the *ouled naïl* or dancing girl, of Biskra is often that described by the prophet Jeremiah: "Though thou clothest thyself with crimson, though thou deckest thee with ornaments of gold, though thou rentest thy face with painting, in vain shalt thou make thyself fair; thy lovers will despise thee" (Jeremiah 3: 30).

## A TRAGEDY WITH A HAPPY ENDING

Early in the morning, as I was examining Guermessa and taking some photographs of the caves, we heard screams, and on turning saw an old woman pitch headlong into the abyss below. She had come out to throw rubbish down the precipice and had lost her balance and toppled over.

She hit the boulders and rebounded like a rubber ball, and brought up at last almost out of sight in the valley below. We all thought she was dead, for a fall of about 900 feet surely meant death, and it seemed as if every bone in her body must have been broken.

Her relatives and family went down to pick up her remains, and two hours later she was brought up, more dead than alive. I expressed my regret to the sheik of the village, and he said she was only a woman and an old one at that, and that her time had come.

This accident darkened my day's enjoyment, and for several days it was a very vivid and unpleasant memory. Imagine my relief on hearing later that she had entirely recovered, and that not a single bone was broken.

From the Troglodyte caves of Guermessa to the valley below, where the springs of drinking water are situated, is a drop of about 1,800 feet. The path is over 3 miles long and zigzags all the way up.

## CAVE-DWELLERS THAT LIVE
## BY THEMSELVES

From Gabes to Dehibat, and from Matmata over the Tripoli border, one finds, scattered here and there, small groups of cave-dwellers living in caves in the mountain side, sometimes only one family.

They build, with great care, water-tight cisterns, for wells and springs are not at all frequent in this country, and rain water is greatly valued for drinking purposes. In some parts there is actually not enough spare water even to brush one's teeth, and I do not believe the animals ever get sufficient to drink.

This condition has naturally led to the introduction of a breed of animals that can live fairly well on very little water.

Last May Brebisch and Mohammed took me to a Troglodyte town perched on the top of a table-land, and here in the bowels of the earth I saw a huge mosque, with great Gothic-like arches carved out of massive rock. Besides having caves in the rocks, they had skyscrapers made of *rhofas* (artificial caves of hardened mud) superposed one upon another to a height of from 8 to 12 stories.

Wild-looking Troglodytes, fully armed, were guarding this stronghold when we rode up, but as the Cadhi was known and greatly loved by my companions, we received a warm welcome.

I was stupidly induced to climb to the top of the *rhofas* to see the remarkable panorama. It seems to me that at last the missing link has been found, for certainly no beings ever climbed as agilely, except monkeys, as did these Troglodytes.

The climbing up was far more simple than the coming down. I longed to be a member of that curious brotherhood of the *Aissaiouas* that jump from great heights without hurting themselves. The little stone steps put in here and there had been worn by centuries of use until they sloped downward and projected only about three or four inches, so one could hardly get a foothold. Undressing as much as I could, throwing my shoes and clothes to the ground, and praying to Allah to guard me in the perilous moments, I descended as best I could, slowly and painfully, but finally in safety.

Photo by Frank Edward Johnson

TUNISIAN MAIDENS OF HIGH RANK

The girl to the right is Mabrucka, the daughter of my host at Foumtatahouine, Mohammed-Es-Seghir, Cadhi of Djebel-El-Abiodth; the other her chum. A photograph of a girl of this class is very rare, as it is usually only those who have no social position to lose who will consent to pose for a picture. In this case, the young ladies being very sure of their place in society, made an exception in honor of my visit.

Photo by Lehnert and Landrock

### AN ARAB MATRON OF MIXED BLOOD

As can be seen by her eyebrows, which meet, she is married. Owing to the conglomeration of tribes in Tunisia and Tripolitania, it is very hard to distinguish between the various races.

Photo by Lehnert and Landrock

THE MOTHER OF AN OULED NAÏL

The women of this tribe, even the older married women, do not, as a rule, wear the veil so universal among other Moslem peoples; instead, the head is bound up in a turban, over which is drawn a sort of white mantle.

Photo by Frechon

IN THE HAREM COURTYARD: TUNIS

Photo by Lehnert and Landrock

## FINE FEATHERS MAKE FINE BIRDS

Nowhere is this proverb more true than in the case of the *ouled naïls*, for they enhance their somewhat scanty natural charms by carefully adorning themselves to the utmost. They affect the gayest of colors and a profusion of jewels; they mix their hair with wool and plaster it with grease, forming great braids, which they loop down over their ears, framing their faces, as it were, in ebony.

There is wild excitement in going over an unknown country and not being sure whether one can bring up at the right place before dark. Heat, thirst, and danger are forgotten in the glorious landscape, with its iridescent colors.

Mohammed and Brebisch were most picturesque, with their great straw hats, about four feet in diameter (see photo, page 4), decorated with embroidered gazelle leather, creamy white silken *bernouses* waving in the wind, and the gaily colored trappings of the Arab saddle and bridle, with solid silver mountings and massive silver stirrups. Mohammed was mounted on a dark-gray Arabian stallion, and Brebisch rode a pure white horse, about five years old and full of spirit.

Each boy carried shotguns and pistols. They did not care where they went and would never take a dare. It was useless to caution them. They would reply that Allah would take care of them, and he certainly did. Brebisch was always humming a weird tune in a minor key, and good-natured, no matter what happened.

In this part of the country messages are sent by runners, very thin, strong, wiry men, without an ounce of fat, who think nothing of a 30-mile run before breakfast.

We usually paused on our journey before the sun became too hot, and ate lunch in the cool of a Troglodyte cave. The lunch always consisted of *cous-cous* (native wheat prepared so that it looks like fine grains of rice), with vegetables when they were to be had—there were never any here—and steamed with a lamb or an entire sheep, cooked whole.

One of my favorite dishes was *chuck-chucks*, made of fried eggs, cooked with oil, and dried red peppers. The bread was always excellent—made of barley or millet. There were always quantities of dried dates at a meal.

## THE DANCE OF THE HAIR

One evening Brebisch came in, all excitement, and said that we were to attend a betrothal ceremony about 9 o'clock.

Walking down by the light of the full moon, we were guided directly to the place by the shrill sounds of the native bagpipes and tom-toms (a species of drum), that were making a fearful din.

In the courtyard of a large *fonduk* (or inn) were gathered together a motley array of Arabs, Sudanese, Berbers, Touaregs, and weird creatures, dressed in the skins of small animals, with frightful, grinning masks, and bones and skulls dangling here and there. They were the dancers from Timbuktu, and were making so much noise that it was impossible even to think.

As we entered a semi-nude figure sprang out at us, howling, jumping, and making contortions; his only garment seemed to be a short skirt, that gave him the ludicrous appearance of a ballet dancer. The men in skins surrounded us, and amidst a deafening noise we were escorted to our seats of honor. Dusky forms had been busy making a great bonfire.

Then began a curious dance, that reminded me in a way of our North American Indian dancers and medicine men. The master of ceremonies went around in turn to each guest, and the bagpipes screeched and the tom-toms beat. Every guest gave coppers or a piece of silver to our host, and this devilish-looking man would spring high into the air, hitting his heels together several times, and spin like a tetotum. He improvised original songs, praising his various guests and their liberality. Judging from the eager expression of the spectators, the words of these songs must have been witty.

THE JEWELS OF AN OULED NAÏL

Here we see one in all her glory. She has necklaces of gold coins, cunningly wrought amulets of gold and silver, innumerable bracelets of fine workmanship, and last. but not least, the wide golden crown of intricate design, embellished with turquoises and coral.

DREAMING OF THE FUTURE

A dancing girl dreaming of the day when she will have accumulated enough in coins and jewels to return to the tents of her tribe as a heavily dowered bride. Most travelers remark upon the passionate fondness of the *ouled naïl* for adornment, but with shrewd business instinct the girls regard their gems both as an attraction for their present profession and a provision for the future.

Photo by Lehnert and Landrock

### A DANCING GIRL OF TOUGOURT, ALGERIA

These *ouled naïl* girls are very dark in complexion, their eyebrows are generally penciled until they meet, and small signs are made on the face by tattooing, as can be seen on the forehead of the girl in the picture. They heighten their charms by a liberal application of grease paint and rouge.

Photo by Bougault

## IN HER ARMOR OF COINS

These necklaces of coins are usually composed of French 20-franc pieces and English sovereigns, as it is the fashion among the patrons of the *ouled naïls*, when particularly pleased with a dance, to toss them gold pieces, which are immediately added to the collection around their necks.

### AT REST AFTER THE DANCE

This *ouled naïl*, with her robe of vivid crimson embroidered in gold, her soft silk veil of the palest blue silk, the wide gold girdle with its innumerable chains and pendants, the necklaces of coins, the bracelets of silver and gold, and the crown-like head-dress, is the personification of the gorgeous East.

NAKHLA, THE PEARL OF THE SAHARA

This is a famous beauty of the *ouled naïl* tribe, Nakhla by name, whose charms are more in accordance with Western taste than those of most reputed beauties of this people. Though belonging to a class regarded as outside respectable society, these girls never depart from what is perfectly proper in the matter of dress, and in the dance they are as fully clothed as in the street.

Photo by Lehnert and Landrock

AN INTERVAL OF REST AND REFRESHMENT

When not engaged in the dance, the *ouled naïl*'s greatest delight is to lounge in the sun—an object of interest and admiration from her bright clothes and her wealth of jewels. These periods of relaxation are invariably enlivened by the cigarette, to which every class of Moorish society is addicted.

At last the noise of the bagpipes ceased, to be taken up by flageolets in a minor key. A row of young women and girls, with long hair falling down their back, had crept in, unnoticed in the dark, and taken up their position between us and the bonfire, so that they stood out like black silhouettes against the flame; all were unveiled. Slowly and gracefully they began to sway and twist their lithe bodies in rhythm to the weird music. Most of the time they danced on their knees, bending and twisting, their hair sometimes standing out almost straight, then falling about their heads.

It was the far-famed "Dance of the Hair," that few foreigners have ever seen. Toward the end of the dance the bonfire of esparto grass was allowed to grow dim, and the women vanished into the night, for clouds had obscured the moon.

I was curious to see the *fiancé* and kept asking Brebisch to point him out to me. About the

THE DANCE OF THE OULED NAÏLS

The dancing of these girls consists of a series of posturings to music quite different to the usual Western idea of a dance. The women take their places to the sound of tom-toms and *derboukas* or pipes, then slowly and langorously they move the body from the waist up, gradually working up to a variety of turnings, twistings, and undulations, all accomplished without moving the feet.

time the "Dance of the Hair" began a dear little boy, not quite four years old (a son of the devil-man), had come over and snuggled close up to me. He was so tired that he fell asleep, but when the bonfire died down he awakened and scampered over to the women, and vanished with them. This small boy was the future bride-groom, and his two-and-a-half-year old *fiancée*, called Machla, which means "The Palm Tree," lived many miles away and could not be pres-

ent at the "Dance of the Hair" on their be-trothal.

## OUR ADVENTURE WITH ALI, THE FINANCIER

On our arrival toward dusk at Foumtata-houine, when my luggage had been taken out of the two-wheeled cart and placed in the house the Cadhi had put at my disposal, I told Ali to go to the *fonduk* (Arab inn) and curry the mule, give it plenty to eat and water it four hours later. He was to spend all his time looking after that mule, for which I felt a great responsibility. The Caid of Medenine had lent it to me, no other animal being available, and it was his pet mule. In certain parts of the Orient a fine mule is preferred to a horse, and costs much more. It lives longer and can pull almost three times as much.

Ali was a worker, Ali was a hustler, Ali was a financier, and he loved animals and took splendid care of his master's mule. After 48 hours'

rest, I told Ali to return to Medenine with the cart and mule.

On my arrival at Foumtatahouine I had told Ali, "You see to the mule and I will pay for its stabling and food. I do not wish the Cadhi to pay one centime."

Ali smiled and showed his white teeth and said, "*Oui, Monsieur,*" in his broken Arab-French.

The Cadhi said, "Now, Ali, Monsieur is my guest and I want to pay for the fodder of his mule."

Photo by Lehnert and Landrock

DANCING GIRLS OF SOUTHERN ALGERIA

In northern Africa the dance does not have the religious significance which invariably accompanies it in India. The dance of the *ouled naïl* is almost as foreign to occidental ideas as is that of the Nautch girl of Benares, and less attractive.

Ali answered, "So be it, Sheik Cadhi."

When Ali arrived in due time at Medenine, he had carried a *Maribout* and his son from Foumtatahouine to Bir-El-Ahmar (the Red Well), and received three francs for that and a free lunch.

On his arrival home he said to his master, "O noble Caid, I took the stranger, as thou didst command me, safely to Foumtatahouine. I cared for thy mule, watered and fed it with care. I remained three times one day at the inn and paid 22 piasters for barley and bran. Sheik Cadhi fed me; therefore, O Caid, thou owest me 22 piasters."

Three times 22 is 66; putting the price of the barley and bran at 12 piasters, Ali made almost 600 per cent, for all three of us paid him in full.

When Mohammed-Es-Seghir, Cadhi of Djebel-El-Abiodth, heard that I had paid and that he had paid, he thought it a huge joke; and, when a week later, we heard that the Caid had also paid, he laughed until the tears rolled down his cheeks.

Many weeks later, when calling on the Caid of Medenine to thank him for his kindness in lending me the mule, and to ask him if it came back in good condition, I asked him,

A TENT TOWN OF SOUTHERN ALGERIA

In southern Algeria there are a number of temporary towns in the desert whose inhabitants dwell wholly in tents. These towns are in existence for about nine months each year, and are inhabited chiefly by Bedouins. In the picture we see such a town, with the groups of tents scattered about on the desert sands. In the foreground some of the inhabitants are watching the dance of two *ouled naïls*.

DANCING IN THE SAND

Europeans come into contact with the famous dancing girls of the *Ouled Naïl* tribe of desert Arabs chiefly at the city of Biskra, in Algeria, where two whole streets are inhabited by women of this class. They resort thither to earn dowries which will enable them to return to the desert and marry men of their own tribe.

"Why do you keep a servant that cheats all three of us?"

He smiled and said, "Ali is fond of horses and mules and gives them the very best of care; if an animal goes lame, he will walk for days rather than hurt it, and he always gives the animals enough to eat. I know that he often buys barley for less than he charges me, but then my stables are well cared for."

### HOLDING AN EARLY MORNING LEVÉE

When I awoke in the morning I was obliged to open the shutters, that I had to keep closed on account of thieves; then the servants, Ben Saada among them, that slept in front of the various doors of my house would hear me and go and call the Cadhi and Mohammed.

In a minute or two they would come in and salute me. Then Kaliphe and Brebisch would next appear, followed by any Troglodyte sheiks that were in the village. These men would sit in solemn array while I would finish my toilet and dress.

When they arrived, in the midst of a sponge bath, it was, to say the least, a bit disconcerting, but the chief interest to them was to watch me shaving and brushing my teeth. Mohammed told me that he had tooth-brushes, but had never seen tooth powder or paste, and, moreover, he never used his brushes. (His teeth, by the way, were superb.)

After my bath, helping hands were not lacking to aid me on with my clothes.

Sometimes my rooms were so crowded that those that could not enter had to look in through the open windows.

Since Mabrucka told me that she and all the women of the harem had come in one day with her elder brother when I was sound asleep after a hard day's ride, I have never been quite certain if there were not peep-holes from some of the harem rooms, and that the fair dames of the various households had not watched me dressing! Who knows!

Every morning after shaving, when I turned to put my hand on my military hair-brushes, they would be missing, and Brebisch and Mohammed would be busy, fez in hand, brushing their caps. Mohammed would say, "*Cher ami*, these brushes are wonderful for smoothing a fez."

My nail-file and scissors were also much appreciated. Every time that Mohammed would cut his finger nails he would spread a towel, napkin, or newspaper to catch all the cuttings. It seems that the hair and nails of fingers and toes belong to the Evil One, and, unless the cuttings are burned or buried in the ground (sand), it gives possession of the living body to the Devil.

Even numbers bring good fortune; odd numbers very bad luck. Five is an exception and a very lucky number. The sudden change in the gait of a horse may lead to the most important decisions.

When the Cadhi started out on his long ride to Tripoli with the other members of the French Commission, he saw seven black crows and he was terribly downcast, but a moment later another crow flew up and joined the seven, making eight all told, and the Cadhi was all smiles and hope.

One must never say, "Tomorrow we will do so and so," or go to such a place; one must first say, "An-cha-Allah," which means "if God wills."

One night after twilight, when squatted in front of our Troglodyte caves, some mighty hunters of the Great Tents (Sahara) told me the following fable:

"A lion of the Sahara, the king of beasts, said to himself, 'An-cha-Allah, tomorrow night I will kill a buffalo with a stroke of my paw and carry it to my cubs. The next day, 'God willing,' I will slay a horse and carry it back. The third day I will kill a calf, 'God willing;' then I will kill a sheep;" but, despising so small a creature as a sheep, the lion omitted to say "An-cha-Allah," and when he killed the sheep, to punish him, God made him drag it on the ground.

And the king of beasts does so even today, so say those hunters of the Great Sahara, and there is no reason to doubt their word.

## WHY THE TROGLODYTES LIVE IN CAVES

Many letters have been written me since the publication of my article on "The Molemen" in the NATIONAL GEOGRAPHIC MAGAZINE of October, 1911, inquiring why the Troglodytes live in caves and do not build houses, asking details of their life and habits, and laying stress on birth, death, and burial.

One man wrote: "If they have no wood or stones to build houses with, why do they not use bricks?" How can they make bricks without mud, or mud without water, and of what use are bricks without cement?

### IN A TUNISIAN STREET

Nowhere in the world does the "Arabian Nights" come home to the traveller so vividly as in North Africa. Here is the changeless East, the same today as it was a thousand years ago, with all its wealth of color, its sunshine and its picturesqueness.

THE FALCONER

In Northern Africa the falcon is still used in the pursuit of game. The bird must always be let slip with the words, "In the name of Allah, the great Allah," otherwise the game seized is not lawful food, as this formula must be pronounced over all animals killed for the table.

AN ARAB AND HIS FLOWER

About the end of June each day at sunset, every Arab, rich or poor, buys a small bunch of jasmine from the itinerant vendors who cry their wares in the streets. The flower is then fastened in the turban over the ear, as shown in the picture.

THE TOMB OF A MARABOUT

In Northern Africa the term *Marabout* has a very wide meaning. It is applied to every man who in any way devotes himself to religion, from dignified and influential scholars of holy life—justly esteemed as saints—to wandering mendicants who subsist on alms or by the sale of spells, charms or other objects of pious superstition.

ALLAH'S GREATEST GIFT—THE DATE PALM

In Northern Africa the date palm is the Queen of Trees, and not for its beauty alone. Its shade is a protection from the heat, its leaves give mats, its fibre ropes, its juice a drink and its fruit is one of the most satisfying and nourishing foods in the world.

IN THE COURTYARD OF AN ARAB HOUSE

Here are some children working in the courtyard of a house in Tunis. The beautifully carved columns are worthy of a museum, as are the antique Moorish tiles always found in the houses of the wealthy classes.

A FLOWER OF THE SAHARA

It is not their beauty alone which makes the Arab girls so attractive to the eye, for their charms are enhanced by the picturesque costumes they wear. These striped garments are of most wonderful colors—pale yellow, green, orange or purple—and often embellished with equally vivid embroidery.

A YOUNG BEDOUIN BEAUTY

In tropical lands children mature very rapidly. The attractive girl in the picture, though only eleven years old, is as much a woman as a child of the North would be at twice her age.

A DAUGHTER OF THE DESERT

The women of the Nomad tribes who wander in the south of Tunisia are singularly beautiful. The characteristic tatooing on the chin and cheeks is not considered to detract from but rather to add to a maiden's charms.

THE INDOOR DRESS OF A TUNISIAN MAID

The clothing worn by the sexes is the exact opposite of that which prevails among western nations, for it is the women who wear trousers while the men wear skirts. Though somber when abroad, the Arab woman is resplendent with color at home, for the richest of silks and the most gorgeous embroidery are none too good for the privacy of the women's apartments.

TWO OULED NAÏLS IN CHARACTERISTIC GARB

The Ouled Naïls are a tribe of desert-Arabs living in Algeria, whose girls resort to the cities to earn money by dancing. As they appear unveiled and bedecked in jewels, they are outside the pale of respectable women. The goldpieces which form their headdress make up their dowry when they return to their tribe to get married.

A ROADSIDE MEETING

Here is a characteristic scene such as can be found in almost any oasis in North Africa. The donkey is ubiqui-
tous as a beast of burden, and, as the traveller in these regions knows, North Africa could be properly called a
land of boys.

### A LAUNDRY MAID OF TUNISIA

A native woman in the Oasis near Gabes ready to return home after having done her washing at the stream. Her dress is caught together by curious safety-pins of a primitive type which have been in use from time immemorial. Note the heavy silver anklets and large earrings.

A BEGGAR OF TRIPOLI

Beggars are numerous in all Moslem countries, and alms are given freely, as the Koran enjoins. There are ways, however, of lawfully avoiding a donation. "In the name of Allah give alms," wails the beggar. "May Allah satisfy all thy wants," says the wealthy man piously—but he passes on.

THE MONEY CHANGER

There is a considerable Hebrew colony in Tunis which is very active in commerce. Though for the most part they have adopted the costume of their Arab neighbors, there are certain little differences in dress by which the members of this race can be distinguished.

Were we Americans to be suddenly placed in a country like theirs, without wood or water, and so far away from the world that importation of these commodities was impossible, we would have to follow the example of the Troglodytes or die of exposure. On these mountain table-lands climatic changes are great, and some sort of dwelling is needed.

The Troglodytes of extreme southern Tunisia speak Berber-Arabic and have adopted the Mohammedan religion.

At an unknown period the ancestors of these Troglodytes of today were all mountain Troglodytes, living on the tops of high table-lands overlooking the surrounding country, usually on sugar-loaf peaks with precipitous sides, so that an enemy could be killed by stones being rolled down upon them.

Driven out of their mountain abodes by the scarcity of food and water, the inhabitants of some of these villages came down to the plains, where they have lived ever since. But, having been accustomed to their cave-dwellings, they preferred them to any other kind, so they built artificial caves, such as we see in Medenine, Metmetemur, and other towns farther south.

THE OASIS

The canal shown here irrigates the oasis and makes it fertile. It takes but a little irrigation to transform a barren stretch of sand into a garden as verdant as the Garden of Eden.

THE MINARET OF THE GREAT MOSQUE: TUNIS

The Mosque of the Olive Tree, founded in 698, is the chief mosque of the city. One of its most attractive features is the handsome minaret of interlaced brickwork shown in the picture. Attached to the mosque is a Moslem university, where about 1,000 youths receive instruction in the Koran and other branches of orthodox learning (see pages 50-51).

These caves not only serve as homes, but also for the purpose of huge storehouses for their food, guns, *gourbis* (tents made of camels' and goats' hair), harnesses, extra ammunition, plows, and other agricultural implements.

## A SEMI-NOMADIC PEOPLE

These people are pastoral, and most of the tribes are nomadic during nine months of the year. Their towns are built in ovals, or small horseshoes, only one entrance for each tribe, so that a few brave men, armed to the teeth, can easily protect their strongholds from thieves. One might say that these Troglodyte towns were the safe-deposit vaults of the cave-dwellers.

Each man has his individual key, which he never forgets to take with him wherever he goes, for if he did, on returning, he would find his cave empty. These keys look something like a banjo handle made of wood. Each key has plugs that fit in it, and no two designs are alike; so that, unless the plugs fit the holes, it would be impossible to unlock the front door.

On the return of a wanderer, he takes his key from one of his saddle-bags and screws or fastens it into a stick that he leaves behind. He then inserts it through a hole to the right of the door and thrusts in his arm, turning the stick at right angles, and scratches the door with the key until he finds the lock. The plugs of the key finally catch into the holes of the lock and, on pulling, the door opens.

## TROGLODYTES THAT BURROW LIKE THE MOLES

The tribes of the Houaia Mountains, comprising the villages of Matmata, Benioussa, Benizelten, and Hadidiji, tired of living on the high table-lands, where climbing up and down was difficult, decided, about a hundred years ago, to come down and live in the valleys.

But wood was lacking and water scarce and it was therefore impossible to build houses, so instead they dug enormous circular holes in the earth. These holes averaged about 27 feet in depth by about 195 feet in circumference. One enters these great courtyards, which are open to the sky, by means of underground tunnels cut out of rock, which is quite soft and can be dug through with a spade, but it hardens on coming into contact with the air (see page 6).

These subterranean caves are so dry that grain will keep indefinitely when stored in them. The dwellings are cool in summer and warm in winter, and out of the way of sand when the sirocco blows.

The people in these underground dwellings live like the patriarchs of old. The head of the family is lord of all he surveys, and lives with his sons and his son's sons, their wives and their children. Frequently almost 100 people live in a single dwelling, each family having their individual cave to themselves.

## TROGLODYTES WHO EMIGRATE

The men of Matmata have more energy than most Arabs. Often two or three adventurous youths receive permission from their fathers (for without that permission they could do nothing) and start on foot or on donkeys for Tunis.

The journey is long. Kairouan, Sacred City of the Sands, is usually visited en route; also the tombs of several celebrated *Marabouts*. Arriving penniless and unknown in Tunis, these young Troglodytes earn money by carrying trunks, running errands, or going to market and carrying vegetables and provisions for housekeepers.

When they have earned enough money to buy two or three copper pots and what looks like a large flower-pot, they hire a small shop, hardly as large as a closet, with an open front facing on the street. Here, about 4 o'clock in the morning, they begin frying cakes in their copper pots, which taste something like apple fritters. These they sell for five centimes, or one cent. The day laborers, going to work, are their patrons.

About 7 o'clock the morning's work is over, and they close the shutters, clean up, and go to sleep. About half past three in the afternoon the shop is again opened. The embers in the flower-pot, which is in reality a stove, are blown by small bellows until they glow, and more fritters are fried. The demand seems greater than the supply.

In about four years' time these young men can lay aside enough money to buy some broad-tail sheep, and goats, and several camels, and return to their native Troglodyte town, where they take to themselves a Troglodyte maid and establish a small but happy home of their own.

## II

## THE UNIVERSITY AT THE MOSQUE OF THE OLIVE TREE IN TUNIS

Few people outside of Tunisia know of the Mohammedan University, where about 1,000 students annually study various branches of history, religion, ethics, and sciences.

Several years ago the students went on strike because the professors came late to their lectures, and some did not turn up at all.

Some of the Arab professors were not particularly interested in the instruction they gave. The students desired a larger curriculum that would include chemistry, physics, physical geography, and several of the modern branches as taught in the smaller American colleges.

The strike was a passive one and lasted about two months. A few of the students were arrested, but almost immediately released. A deputation of students called upon the Bey and the Resident of Tunis and begged them to look into the matter.

The Tunisian government answered that from henceforth the professors would be forced to attend their lecture courses punctually, and that if sufficient funds could be raised some of the modern courses would be adopted by the University of the Olive Tree.

The university headquarters are in the interior of the Grand Mosque of the Olive Tree, so that no foreigner can ever catch a glimpse of it, owing to the mosque belonging to the Malachite rite, where only persons going to pray are allowed to enter (see page 51). Even the *Sheik ül Islam* (a Moslem ecclesiastic occupying in northern Africa a position corresponding to that of the Pope in the Roman Catholic Church) could not grant me permission to enter, although he was most desirous of my seeing the mosque, university, and its various branches. It was suggested by some of my Arab friends that I slip in dressed as an Arab, but this seemed to me a very improper proceeding and I refused to do so.

A Mohammedan society has been formed for the betterment of all classes. This society is known as the *Khaldoúnia.* Wealthy Arab gentlemen volunteer their services as instructors, each one teaching his particular subject. The *Khaldoúnia* has met with tremendous popularity.

Photo by Lehnert and Landrock

ENTRANCE OF THE MOSQUE OF THE OLIVE TREE: TUNIS

This mosque is reputed to be very beautiful, but no European is allowed to enter it or even to inspect the university which is connected with it. Set in a deep niche on one side of the door can be seen the large sign, on which is written in English, French, German, and Italian the warning, "This mosque is reserved for Moslem worship. Entrance forbidden."

## A STREET AT TETUAN

Northern Africa, notwithstanding political divisions, is very similar everywhere. Here is a picture taken in Tetuan, a city of Morocco, nearly a thousand miles distant from Tunis, yet its architecture, its pavements, its veiled women, and hooded men are the same in almost every detail as those found in Tunis.

IN A BISKRA STREET

Biskra is a town in Algeria, situated in an oasis of the Sahara, some three miles long by about one mile broad. The houses in the native quarter are built of hardened mud, with doors and roofs of palm wood. There is also a fine modern town, which is a favorite winter resort for French and other European visitors.

Photo by Lehnert and Landrock

ARAB WOMEN OF ALGIERS

Here is a picture taken at the entrance of a cemetery to which Moslem women resort once a week, usually on Fridays, the Moslem Sabbath. On the day of the weekly visit the cemeteries are by no means gloomy places; all men are excluded, and the ladies, laying aside their veils, indulge in impromptu picnics, with much laughter and gossip.

Photo by Lehnert and Landrock

THE WINDOWS OF THE HAREM

The windows so heavily latticed and barred show how jealously the Moslem guards the privacy and seclusion of his women folk. This seclusion is accepted by the women as a visible sign of their husbands' love and they would strongly resent any evidence of carelessness on his part in this respect.

A MORESQUE BEAUTY

The term Moresque is applied to those Moslems of mixed blood who are found chiefly in the cities on the North African coast. In their veins flows the blood of Roman, Berber, Arab, Spanish, and often other Christian ancestors, and many of their women are strikingly handsome.

AN ARAB DOOR

The Arabs have always expended much artistic care upon the doors of their homes. Wherever the Arab civilization has dominated, as far to the west as Tangier, to the east as Bagdad, and to Zanzibar in the south, these beautifully carved brass-studded portals can be found at the entrance to the houses of the wealthy.

Photo by Lehnert and Landrock

A BAZAR IN TUNIS

The bazars, or *souks*, of Tunis are narrow, winding streets, some of them vaulted and many covered in with a roof of boards. There are five chief bazars; el-Attarin, the market of perfumery; el-Farashin, of carpets and cloths; el-Serajin, of saddlery, and el-Birka, of jewelry. The Souk-el-Birka was formerly the slave market.

Photo by Lehnert and Landrock

THE RITUAL OF GREETING

"No matter the state of one's birth, or power, or dignity, he that is on horseback should greet the man on foot. . . . A man on horseback should speak first to the man he meets riding a mule. A man on a mule should greet first a poor man riding a donkey. . . . These rules of etiquette are most scrupulously kept" (see text, page 93).

Photo by Lehnert and Landrock

IN THE INN

Here are two Arabs from the South resting in their room in the *fonduk*, or inn. The man on the left is holding his rosary or prayer beads. These rosaries are very much in evidence among the Arabs and are—among the wealthier classes—usually made of amber.

They have comfortable reading-rooms, an auditorium, and a small but excellent library. The members meet frequently and discuss all sorts of questions.

## MODERN EDUCATION IN TUNIS

During the past ten years a school for Arab girls has been founded and has met with great success. The head of it is a French woman, who thoroughly understands Mohammedan ways.

No effort is made to proselytize or influence them in any way; the desire is simply to make these young girls intelligent and useful members of the community, so that when they marry they may have attractive homes and be intelligent companions to their husbands. They are taught plain, common-sense sewing, hygiene, common-sense cooking, how to set a table properly, to read and write; also arithmetic and bookkeeping.

The school is very largely attended by the daughters of the aristocrats and wealthy families. The Arabs are taking much interest in the school, and its headquarters have had to be changed several times since it was started, so all its scholars could be housed.

The French have made public instruction compulsory throughout Tunisia, and even in the far-away Troglodyte villages small schools are to be found, which as a rule are attended only by the boys, but some of the broad-minded and intelligent Arabs are sending their daughters. These public schools have both Arab and French instructors, who teach history, geography, reading, writing, and arithmetic.

The Arab teacher instructs the natives in the Koran and in reading and writing Arabic. The Koran is not only a religious book, but it contains excellent advice on daily life that is quite practical. When an Arab boy has learned to read the Koran, he is an excellent Arab scholar.

The result of these public schools is that the younger generation can speak, read, and write excellent French, whereas most of the older men do not understand a word.

The French government has allowed the natives absolute independence of thought and religion. In the far-off Troglodyte towns, where no mosques existed, some have been built by the government. This has been a very wise move, because it has endeared the French to the hearts of the Tunisians.

Justice is administered to the natives according to the ancient laws of the country. A foreigner, be he French, Italian, or English, is judged by a French court, just as if he were in France.

The Oriental mind cannot quite grasp the French (Roman) laws, and this native and French dual tribunal is most effective in dealing with justice. The law is swift, just, and severe. Evil-doers are always caught and punished, so that from the lowest to the highest there is strict law and order.

Tunisia has a French and Arab police and mounted police, called *oüdjac*, that patrol the country (see page 4).

## III
## CONCERNING THE CAMEL AND THE LOCUST

There are almost as many varieties of camels as horses. The Arab name for camel is *djemel*. Those of Tunisia, Tripolitania, and Algeria have one hump and are really dromedaries. Certain breeds of camels can withstand the great heat of the Sahara Desert and others that of the zero weather of Tibet and China.

THE STREET OF THE ANDALUSIANS: TUNIS

This is a typical quiet street in the older part of the city of Tunis—narrow, tortuous, and in places vaulted over, while under foot are the age-resisting but uncomfortable cobblestones

Photo by Lehnert and Landrock

THE WATER SELLER

Here is a picture of an itinerant water seller taken in the streets of Tripoli of Barbary. The water is carried today in a skin just as it has been from time immemorial.

ARAB FALCONERS

Throughout northern Africa hunting with falcons is a favorite sport with the native Arab population. The female of the peregrine falcon is the best bird for purposes of the chase, representing the highest and most courageous type of all the birds of prey (see also page 33).

The ordinary camels of northern Africa (dromedaries) cost from 150 to 300 francs (30 to 60 dollars) apiece, and they live on almost anything that they can find to eat by the roadside; hence it costs next to nothing for their native Arab owners to keep them. Should a European own camels and attempt to feed them with hay and grain, he would find that they ate a great deal, and that it would cost at least a dollar a day for each one.

During the Italian war in Tripoli the usual price for hiring a camel and its driver to take food supplies from Ben Garden to the Turkish camp was from 3 to 3½ francs a day (60 to 70 cents). Between Kairouan and Sbeitla are many miles of bad land, where almost nothing thrives save the prickly pear. This has been cultivated by the natives, is rented out in great tracts, and has become a source of comfortable income.

It is amazing to see the rapidity with which a herd of 500 camels will eat to the ground a large pasturage of prickly pear from 8 to 10 feet high. Leaves, stems, prickles and all, disappear like magic.

HOW THE CAMEL'S HUMP GETS FAT

Throughout southern Tunisia and Algeria the natives keep all their date stones and give

THE JEWISH CEMETERY: TUNIS — Photo by Lehnert and Landrock

Tunis has a very ancient Jewish colony, numbering some 50,000 souls, many of whom are descended from families which settled at Carthage before the destruction of Jerusalem by Titus in A. D. 70. Though both sexes wear a special costume, that of the men is with difficulty distinguishable from that of their Moslem neighbors; but the high sugar-loaf cap and all-enveloping cloak render the Jewish woman at once apparent.

them to exhausted camels, weary from their long Sahara march.

The camel resists at first, and the date stones, moistened in a little water, are pushed forcibly, by the handful, down the camel's throat, after it has been made to kneel, and then securely fastened. In two or three days the camel learns to eat them of its own accord. The natives say that these date stones make the hump of the camel strong and stiff.

The camel in its long march across the Sahara frequently finds very little to eat and lives on the fat of its own hump. When this continues during a long time, the hump of the camel becomes flabby and almost disappears. The African broad-tailed sheep lives in the same way on the fat of its own tail.

The flesh of a camel is eaten by the natives throughout the Sahara and northern Africa. The greatest delicacy is the hump, which contains a great deal of fat. One can always tell the condition of the animal by observing its hump. When a camel is weary, after a long march across the Sahara, its hump almost disappears, whereas when it starts out on a journey the hump is well defined.

Camels of Tunisia, Algeria, and Tripolitania are used almost entirely as beasts of burden, although in Tunisia one occasionally sees them drawing two-wheeled carts, or plowing. The usual weight of the burdens carried by a camel varies from 550 to 600 pounds; this is the average for the camels going from town to town along the coast or the borders of the Sahara.

Should they be planning to cross the Sahara, the weight of the burden would be less, as the strain of the month's journey through the desert is tremendous. The usual march when crossing the desert is 30 kilometers a day (about 20 miles), with an occasional day's rest.

When a camel is being ladened it keeps up a continual snarling, and should it be overburdened it refuses to arise.

Most camels are vicious and their bite is very dangerous. Hardly a week passes at the large native hospital in Tunis but some unfortunate camel driver dies of blood poisoning caused by a camel's bite.

The grinding motion of a camel's jaw crushes to pulp whatever it bites; so that the arm or leg has to be amputated, and blood poisoning usually sets in before the patient can reach the hospital.

The ordinary camel would have difficulty in crossing the desert unless it were born and bred in it, and it would be folly for a man setting out on such a journey to select camels that were unused to the desert. The probabilities are that his caravan would never reach its journey's end.

Great care must be taken in selecting beasts of burden for a caravan trip across the Sahara, and camels must be secured at towns in the desert, where Sahara camels, accustomed to the great wastes of sand, are obtainable. Those bred near the coast have become more or less accustomed to drinking at frequent intervals and require water every two or three days. Those of the Sahara can go much longer without water

and do not suffer in the least. A camel can abstain from drinking for six to ten days during the winter, spring, and autumn. In the hot summer months of July, August, September, and October, five days' abstinence seem to be the limit without inflicting unnecessary suffering upon the animal.

## SUPERB RACING CAMELS OF THE DESERT

In the interior of northern Africa is a superb race of camels known as the *mehara* (singular, *mehari*), or racing camels. The *mehara* owe a great deal to the care taken in their breeding during the past 2,000 years. Ancient writers speak of camels used by the army of Xerxes, more than 2,000 years ago, that had the speed of the fastest horses; these were doubtless *mehara*.

When a baby *mehari* is born it is swathed in bandages to prevent the stomach from getting too large, and is taken into the family tent, where it is nursed and watched over with care and tenderness. When a year old, it is sheared, and is known from then on as a *bou-keutaa*, which means "the father of the shearing." Arabs are very fond of nicknames and everything and everybody is given one.

For the first year it is allowed to wander at will and follow its mother. The *bou-keutaa* is weaned by a pointed stick being run through one nostril and left in the wound. When the young camel tries to suckle its mother the stick pricks her and she kicks the baby camel away. It soon leaves the mother and learns to eat fresh green shrubs. In the spring it is sheared again and the name of *heug* replaces that of *bou-keutaa*.

When it is two years old its training begins. A halter is placed around the head and a cord tied to one of the fore feet. It is kept quiet first by gestures and the voice; later by the voice

A JEWISH BEAUTY OF TUNIS

Photo by Lehnert and Landrock

Throughout northern Africa beauty and fat are thought to be the same and nowhere is this more true than in the Jewish colony in Tunis. This gaudy costume, the satin breeches, the pink silk jacket covered with embroidery in silk and gold thread, the tall sugar-loaf cap, and the curious slippers ending under the instep, while still common, is slowly but surely giving place to the ordinary Paris fashions.

A HOME IN TUNIS

Photo by Lehnert and Landrock

This courtyard, in an Arab home in Tunis, is a remarkably fine specimen of Moorish architecture. The capitals and columns are of marble, antique Moorish tiles ornament the walls, while the arches are of hand-carved stucco-work of Arab design. On the second floor a balcony runs round all four sides of the court, and the women's apartments open on to it.

Photo by Lehnert and Landrock

A MOONLIGHT EFFECT IN THE COURTYARD

The courtyard of this Moorish house by moonlight brings home to us the charm and mystery of the East. The delicate pillars of the court, the rich tile-work of the walls, the sleeping figures, and the moonlight make up a picture such as Haroun-al-Raschid must have seen when seeking the adventures recounted in the "Arabian Nights."

alone. Then the cord is loosened, but should it make a step it is tied again. Finally it understands what is required, but the lessons are only terminated when it will stand in one place without moving for an entire day.

To make a *heug* kneel, the rider cries out, "Ch-ch-ch," and a person standing near strikes it with a stick on the knees at the same time the rider speaks to it. The camel soon learns to kneel without being struck. To make it a fast runner, the rider whips it on both flanks alternately with a rhinoceros-hide whip and cries out in Arabic to excite it. A young *mehari* is very fond of its own skin, and on being struck starts on a gallop. The whipping keeps up and the camel tries to get away by running faster. The long legs seem like wings and it flies past with the speed of an ostrich. It will stop instantly at a pull on the rein, no matter what speed it has been making.

When the rider jumps off, or should he happen to fall, a well-trained *mehari* will stand quite still and wait, while should the master happen to be injured the faithful beast will never leave him.

When a *heug* can turn in a narrow circle around a spear and start off at full speed the instant it is pulled up, the period of training is considered finished. The camel is no longer a *heug*, it has become a *mehari* and is ready for the races or the war-path.

### THE WAY TO RIDE A RACING CAMEL

A *mehari* is never used as a beast of burden; all it ever carries is a saddle (something like a Mexican saddle, made of gazelle skin, dyed red, with a high pommel and a cross in front), two saddlebags, and a rider.

The rider is buckled into the saddle by two belts. His feet are crossed in front of the saddle and rest on the neck of the *mehari*. His slippers are usually slung across the pommel, and the *mehari* is guided by the wriggling of the rider's toes.

An iron ring passes through one nostril of the animal and a rein of camels' hair is attached. Should the *mehari* nibble from the bushes on the wayside, the slightest jerk of the rein will bring it up, and a pull to the right or left will make it take the direction wished, although the voice and the toes are the usual guides. The nostrils of the *mehari* are as sensitive as those of a bull and the least pressure of the rein insures obedience.

The wives of the rich caids and sheiks travel on *mehara* and are hidden from the gaze of mankind by the curtains of ornate palanquins.

The *mehara* are used entirely by the Arabs when on the war-path, or *razzia*. Arab friends have told me how caravans in the Sahara have gone many days' journey to reach a certain oasis, to find, on arriving, that the water had all been used by previous caravans and the springs dry.

To run short of water half way across the Sahara is a very serious proposition, which the natives overcome by killing a *djemel*, or ordinary camel, and drinking its blood, after it has cooled and the froth at the top, which the Arabs claim is very poisonous, is skimmed off. The water found in the camel's stomach is also drunk, and, thanks to the blood and the water, the caravan can continue to an oasis further on, where springs of water are found.

### A TERRIBLE CUSTOM

A terrible custom used to prevail among certain tribes of the Sahara. Before starting on a *razzia*, or war-path, old camels of not much value were kept from drinking as long as possible, and just before starting out were allowed to drink their fill; then, according to the Arabs, their tongues were cut or torn out. I think I misunderstood their words. They may have meant that certain nerves or tendons were cut. Without the use of these tendons of the tongue it was impossible for the camels to use the water in their stomachs, but they could live for a long time. When drink and meat were needed, one or two of these camels were slaughtered, the flesh eaten, and the water and blood drunk.

When the camels were killed, the horses are said to have pawed the ground in their eagerness to eat some of the fresh meat. I have never witnessed this cruel treatment of the camels, nor the conduct of the horses, however, and cannot vouch for the truthfulness of these statements, but some French generals of my acquaintance have confirmed them.

IN THE MARKET-PLACE

The market of a North African town is always the place of greatest interest to the traveler: the brilliance of the semi-tropical sun, the quaint houses, the heavily turbaned Moors in their snowy *bernouses*, the blind beggars, the public writers, and an occasional *marabout*, clad, like John the Baptist, in camel's hair, are objects of never-ceasing interest to the Western eye.

Living or dead, a camel is wealth to its master. To the Arabs of the Sahara a camel is like a reindeer to the Laplanders. Living, it carries the tents and provisions. It fears neither hunger, thirst, nor heat; its hair makes their tents (*gourbis*) and *bernouses*; the milk of the female nourishes rich and poor, enriches the dates, and fattens the horses. Its skin makes water-bottles (*mezad*) in which water never becomes cloudy from the action of wind or sun, and shoes and boots with which one can tread without danger on a viper, and protect the feet from the terrible burns made by the sands of the desert when one is barefooted.

A *mehari* on the war-path can save three men. Two ride it and the third takes hold of its tail and is pulled along. The latter changes places with the riders at intervals. When a war-party has lost so many camels that there remains but one camel for every three men, it always retreats.

*Mehara* are usually fawn-colored, with soft, intelligent eyes. They have pointed ears like a gazelle's. Their chests are very well developed,

GROCERY STORES IN TUNIS

Photo by Garrigues

In Tunis those who trade in the same wares keep their shops all together in a single street; thus one street is entirely devoted to grocery stores, another to perfume sellers, and so on. Notice the Arab lady with her heavy black veil.

and they have a small girth, almost like that of a greyhound. Their slender legs bulge with muscles as hard as steel. There is not a pound of superfluous flesh on the entire body.

When at full speed a *mehari* has a most remarkable single-foot or pacing step, the motion of which is not at all disagreeable, and it can cover quite easily 100 miles in a day without undue fatigue. The feet of camels and *mehara* act on the sand like snowshoes on snow. They spread out and prevent the animal from sinking in too deeply. Camels, and *mehara* es-

pecially, prefer the soft sand to traveling on macadamized roads.

The camel is the only animal I know of that eats esparto grass as it grows. Horses, mules, and donkeys are very fond of it when it has been made into hay, but they would die of starvation rather than eat it green. Camels also eat the leaves of the prickly pear, thorns and all. When a *mehari* returns to the tent of its owner in the Sahara, exhausted from a long journey, the women feed it on camels' milk in which has been mixed pulverized dates.

CHILDREN OF THE SOUTH

Photo by Lehnert and Landrock

These children—half Arab, half negro—are descendants of negro slaves from the west coast of Africa. "The French have made public instruction compulsory throughout Tunisia, and even in the far-away Troglodyte villages small schools are to be found, which as a rule are attended only by boys, but some of the broad-minded and intelligent Arabs are sending their daughters. . . . The result of these public schools is that the younger generation can speak, read, and write excellent French, whereas most of the older men do not understand a word" (see text, page 61).

An ordinary camel lives, on an average, to be about 18 years old, a *mehari* from 25 to 30, the 12 extra years being probably due to the better care.

## A PLAGUE OF LOCUSTS IN ALGERIA

Last year Tunisia and Tripolitania were free of that dreadful scourge, the locust (*Schistocerca peregrina*). These creatures resemble large, green grasshoppers, and are from three to four inches long, with red legs and iridescent wings, which make a loud noise as the swarm flies past. Often the sun is obscured for hours at a time, the locusts being hundreds deep and flying at a height of from 15 to 50 feet, and on alighting they have been known to stop a train.

It is impossible for any one that has not seen a plague of locusts to realize their size and

A PRIMITIVE MILL                    Photo by Lehnert and Landrock

This is a typical mill for grinding cereals, such as is found all over North Africa, the motive power being fur-
nished by the mule, that can be dimly discerned in the darkness. The Arab owner did not want to be photo-
graphed, so he threw his *bernous* over his head at the critical moment.

numbers and the horrors of living for weeks at
a time in a country where locusts fly into your
face, enter your house, and even drop into your
food.

Friends of ours had a great place, about 20
miles from Oran, considered one of the most
fertile plantations of Algeria, and our first visit
there showed acres upon acres of vineyards, cultivated as far as the eye could reach, toward the
Mountain of the Lions; golden grain with ears
so full that the stalks could hardly stand up-

right; lemon groves with their yellow fruit and
fragrant blossoms; great groves of mandarins
and oranges, so verdant, so beautiful, and so fertile it seemed like the Garden of Eden.

A south wind blew, and the locusts came.
They were probably the same sort as in the days
of Pharaoh and the plague. At first they came
in small swarms. Men, women, and children
were impressed to help battle against this terrible foe, for wherever the locusts alight nothing green remains when they pass on.

LADIES IN STREET COSTUME: TUNIS

"During the past ten years a school for Arab girls has been founded and has met with great success. The head of it is a French woman, who thoroughly understands Mohammedan ways. No effort is made to proselytize or influence them in any way; the desire is simply to make these young girls intelligent and useful members of the community, so that when they marry they may have attractive homes and be intelligent companions to their husbands" (see text, page 61).

IN THE MOSQUE AT TLEMCEN

This picture shows the *mihrab*, or small niche, found in every mosque, to indicate the direction of Mecca, and to it all the worshipers turn for prayer. This view is taken in the mosque of Sidi Bou Medine, the chief one in Tlemcen, a large city of Algeria.

A FENCE OF PRICKLY PEAR
Photo by Lehnert and Landrock

From Morocco to Egypt the prickly pear, or Barbary fig (*Opuntia ficus indica*) is used to form the hedges. "It is amazing to see the rapidity with which a herd of 500 camels will eat to the ground a large pasturage of prickly pear from 8 to 10 feet high. Leaves, stems, prickles and all, disappear like magic" (see text, page 64).

The fertile plain, rich vineyards, and verdure are in a few hours turned into a barren desert, with only stumps and tree trunks with the leaves gone and the bark all off.

It was a curious sight to see hundreds of Arab and Spanish laborers, overseers, and even wealthy French land-owners themselves, and semi-naked Arab children walking abreast in an almost straight line, each beating an old wooden pail, an empty box, a vegetable can, or a drum and blowing a tin trumpet or twirling a policeman's rattle. Each person or child walks in a furrow to himself, and the deafening noise keeps the locusts from settling. Frequently the owners of the plantations build fires and make them smoke to keep away the swarms of locusts.

When the locusts have alighted late in the afternoon, nothing can drive them off. They take wing the following morning, shortly after sunrise, unless the time has arrived for the female locust to lay her eggs.

### THE NYMPHS OF THE LOCUSTS
### MORE DESTRUCTIVE THAN THE LOCUST

The females excavate holes in the earth two and three inches deep, in which they deposit from sixty-two to sixty-eight eggs, enveloped in a glutinous secretion, shaped somewhat like an ear of wheat.

Men have to plow and spade every inch of ground, for the nymphs are more destructive than the locusts, and the only way to prevent the eggs from hatching is to uncover them and leave them in the sun.

The period of incubation is twenty-one days; then tiny creatures—called nymphs—crawl out. They remain quiet for two days and then begin to eat. They eat and eat and eat.

Men with torches burn the nymphs by the millions, but they crawl out of the earth faster than the hand of man can destroy them. The first one to come out takes the lead, and the others follow in swarms many feet wide. They make a curious noise, like the sound of the sea.

It seems incredible that a thing so small and insignificant is so difficult to destroy. Build great fires and the swarms of crawling, wriggling nymphs will smother them, those in front being burned by millions, and those in the rear pushing on and passing over the burned bodies of the leaders. They will block and fill up a sluggish African stream, and the millions in the rear will pass over unharmed.

The government sends troops to aid in the defense, for it means ruin and starvation to thousands of people, besides heavy money losses. Great trenches are dug and the nymphs fall in, and when three-fourths full kerosene oil is poured on them and they are set afire, or else earth is thrown on them to a depth of about two feet. They can crawl out of the earth if only covered with a few inches, but when deeply covered they smother to death.

The young locusts are most destructive, selecting the choicest vegetables or tender shoots and green leaves. It takes weeks for them to develop from a tiny, black nymph into a full-sized locust, but they increase rapidly in size, and one can almost see their legs and wings develop.

### LOCUSTS AS A FOOD

Saint John the Baptist is spoken of as having lived on locusts and wild honey. From the earliest times the tribes that dwelt on or near the great deserts of Persia, Arabia, and Africa have eaten dried locusts as food, and they will keep on doing so as long as huge swarms fly out of the desert.

Arabs eat the flesh of locusts when killed by themselves, but refrain if their death has been caused by cold or the hand of an infidel, as they are then considered impure. Locusts are eaten after the legs, wings, and heads have been picked off.

They are either grilled or boiled and prepared with native wheat. If dried in the sun they are ground to powder and mixed with goats' or camels' milk and cooked in fat or butter and salt. Almost every animal devours locusts; even camels appear to like them as food.

Mohammed, the Prophet, said: "Allah permits the Arabs to eat only two kinds of animals without cutting their throats—fishes and grasshoppers," and when asked by a friend if he liked locusts, Mohammed replied: "I wish that I had a large basketful to eat immediately."

Photo by Lehnert and Landrock

A LITTLE BEDOUIN GIRL

On her head and body she wears a piece of old sacking as a protection against the winter winds, which are often piercingly cold, even in the Sahara. Her only other garment is a single piece of cloth, which she wears draped round her body somewhat after the fashion of a Roman toga.

Photo by Lehnert and Landrock

A BOY OF THE EXTREME SOUTH

The Arabs of the extreme south of Tunisia are very poor. Here we see an Arab boy clad in his one garment, made of old sacking. Despite his rags, he seems to be enjoying his meal of rich golden-yellow dates, fresh plucked from the palm.

Photo by Bougault

A TYPICAL SCENE IN ONE OF THE LARGER OASES OF NORTHERN AFRICA

"The beautiful oases of southern Tunisia are as near an approach to the Garden of Eden as one can hope to find. Almost everything thrives that can be grown in a semi-tropical country, owing to the rich soil and abundance of water" (see text, page 122).

THE OASIS OF CHENINI, TUNIS    Photo by Lehnert and Landrock

This oasis, near Gabes, is extremely fertile and contains hundreds of thousands of palm trees, which bear a rather poor quality of dates. The oasis is irrigated by the small stream in the foreground.

Arab friends told me the following legend: "The Virgin Mary, Meriem Beut Omran (Mary, the daughter of Omran), as she is called in Arabic, prayed Allah to give her flesh that contained no blood; so Allah sent locusts."

A French officer in Tunisia told me the following story that illustrates the Arab character:

An Arab Caid sowed one of his large fields with wheat. When it was ripe and ready for harvesting, swarms of locusts arrived and devoured every green thing. The Caid watched the locusts eating, and improvised a poem, without trying to drive them away. When my friend saw him he asked the Caid if it were true that the field had been planted with wheat.

"Yes," answered the Caid, "but swarms of locusts arrived, armed with pitchforks (legs) like the gleaners. They have gleaned everything and have not left a thing. Praise be to Allah, who permits such a small and feeble animal to destroy everything!"

## IV
## IN TRIPOLI OF BARBARY

Tripoli of Barbary has an area of about 400,000 square miles. The capital, Tripoli, is one of the most Oriental towns on the Mediterranean, and combines a mixture of Moorish and Turkish architecture.

The low, flat-roofed houses resemble those of Tunisia, but, instead of being creamy white, the Turkish population have painted them red, pink, orange, or blue. The numerous minarets of the mosques are round and have graceful, pointed spires, covered with copper, that glisten in the sun.

Before the Italians took possession, the population consisted of about 1,200 foreigners, including Italians, Maltese, Greeks, French, English, and Germans, and over 36,000 native Turks, Arabs, Berbers, and Sudanese.

An extremely high stuccoed wall of stone and cement, many feet in thickness, encircles the town of Tripoli like a half-moon. It was built to keep out the wild tribes of the Sahara and has aided the Italians in protecting the city on three sides. The wall only stops on reaching the emerald and sapphire waters of the Mediterranean (compare page 2).

Tripoli lacks a natural harbor, but there is a series of great boulders and rock islands that would enable the government to build, for less than $1,000,000, a splendid harbor where the largest steamers would be safe. Now when Neptune is angry all sailing ships and steamers have to leave the harbor and put out to sea.

Small craft, with raking masts and huge lateen sails, anchored in the harbor, remind one of the Barbary pirates that less than a century ago were the dread of all Europe.

Other picturesque boats are those of the Greek sponge fishers, that under full sail resemble huge "Portuguese men-of-war" or *Physalia*, a curious species of jellyfish that floats on the water and raises at will a thin membrane that acts as a sail. One sees them in summer near the coast of North Africa and in the tropical waters of the Atlantic Ocean near the Canary and Cape Verde Islands. Their iridescent colors make them a thing of beauty, but their sting, which is like an electric shock, often proves fatal to the swimmer.

### THE GREEK SPONGE DIVERS

The sponge divers come from Greece and are men of superb physique. Their calling is a difficult and dangerous one. In civilized countries the limit of depth for diving is placed somewhere around 130 feet, but here it is not unusual for them to work at from 180 to 200 feet under water, and the pressure is, of necessity, enormous.

The sum paid to each diver on his arrival from Greece is 6o pounds sterling ($300). After he has gathered enough sponges to pay for the money advanced him, he works on a commission, and each sponge that he brings up nets him a few cents.

After toiling weeks and accumulating a large quantity of sponges, it behooves the diver to have a brother or friend to manage the pump for him on the diving boat; otherwise the captain has been known to pinch the air tube. Pressure for a few seconds suffices, and the diver is pulled aboard, dead.

The commissions and the profits in the sponges go into the pocket of this unscrupulous Shylock, and another "accident owing to tremendous pressure" is reported to the authorities of Tripoli!

These divers are a jolly, happy-go-lucky set of young men, hardly more than boys, who spend their money freely. "Let us enjoy life while we live" is their motto.

They are hard workers and nothing daunts them. They remain under the water as long as the human frame can stand the pressure.

Instead of being pulled up, as divers usually are, they inflate their rubber diving suits by letting the air accumulate instead of escaping and rise to the surface with great rapidity, almost shooting out of the water. This sudden change in atmospheric pressure often causes paralysis and apoplexy, so that on most of the boats there are at least half a dozen crippled divers recovering from this kind of paralysis.

The Greek government in days gone by tried to render aid by sending over two well-equipped hospital ships, but the owners of the diving boats resented this interference and hoisted the Turkish flag, thus preventing the hospital ships from being of service. After two years of fruitless effort on the part of the government, the effort was given up.

## THE SPONGE DIVERS AT PLAY

On Sundays and legal holidays the divers, dressed in their holiday clothes, enjoy life as best they can in the little town of Tripoli, where theaters and even cinematographs are unknown. One of their favorite pastimes is to hire Berber horses and race at full tilt up and down the desert just outside the walls of Tripoli, a harmless pleasure and most amusing to onlookers, for they are poor riders and usually fall off.

At night they go to some native house, where, in the patio, or large rectangular courtyard, brilliantly illuminated with incandescent lights, they sit about long tables and drink coffee or beer. Six or eight blind musicians play weird strains in a minor key, while man after man gets up and dances a *pas seul*. The steps are indescribable, but always graceful. They rarely become intoxicated, and toward midnight they go home.

## THE SPONGE INDUSTRY

The sponges are dried, cleaned, and sent to France and England, where they bring good prices. An ordinary sponge takes about five years to grow and costs from 8 to 20 francs ($1.60 to $4). The Biological Laboratory at Sfax, on the coast of Tunisia, is making a study of the diseases and artificial propagation of sponges, as their ruthless destruction over the coast of northern Africa bids fair to exterminate this industry in a very few years. Great progress has been made in these investigations.

Photo by Lehnert and Landrock

THE ROAD BETWEEN THE GARDENS

"Were the gardens of the oases owned by Europeans and cultivated with modern methods, the result would be phenomenal. Unfortunately, the Arab owners of the oases are not fond of hard work, and content themselves with comparatively little" (see text, page 122).

Photo by Lehnert and Landrock

A QUIET CORNER IN A GARDEN OF EDEN

"A Frenchman has a trial garden where one-half is planted by the old Arab method, the other half according to the latest American and French agricultural methods. He also uses chemical fertilizers, for this particular garden has been cultivated since the Roman occupation, and the ground probably has never been fertilized. The result of his work appears like magic. Palm trees planted four years ago and fertilized have grown as large as Arab palm trees ten years old" (see text, pages 120, 122).

It was my good fortune to be in Tripoli while the Turkish and French commissioners were settling the boundary question between Tripoli and Tunisia, and they enabled me to take some delightful excursions with them to various oases in Tripolitania.

The different consulates were on friendly terms with each other, and all vied in lavishing hospitality upon us. Three days in the week were holidays, Friday being the equivalent of our Sunday for the Mohammedans, Saturday the Jewish Sabbath, and Sunday the Christian Day of Rest.

In the evening, after dinner, we would often stroll down and take a cup of Turkish coffee at a café overlooking the bay, while the waves rolled in at our feet and the stars shown like electric lights in a blue-black sky. The Oriental town about us seemed asleep, but the distant beating of tom-toms and the shrill notes of bagpipes, or flageolets, that occasionally reached our ears showed that somewhere a fête was taking place.

The *souks*, or bazars, of Tripoli are not re-markable, but are interesting nevertheless. The *souks* of the silversmiths are composed entirely of Jews. One never sees an Arab silversmith or blacksmith.

## THE EFFECT OF THE HALLEY COMET ON JEWS AND ARABS

Rain water is the only drinking water used and is kept in huge cisterns built under the houses. During the passing of the Halley comet the Jews of Tripoli were afraid of dying and took refuge in their great cisterns, which they had pumped dry for the purpose. Twenty-four hours having elapsed, they came out of their hiding places to find the world the same as before.

The Arabs said that they were in the hands of Allah and refused to take refuge in their cis-terns. So the few foreigners and the Arabs were the only ones that had any drinking water left, and the Arabs sold drinking water to the Jews until the next rains, about six months later.

A FIELD OF DAISIES IN AN OASIS OF TUNISIA

The wild flowers of the north of Tunisia are so beautiful during the months of February, March, and April that they constitute a distinct attraction in themselves and are responsible for many visitors during this period.

## THE HOUSES OF TRIPOLI

From the street the houses look like great painted or whitewashed walls, with here and there a small iron-barred window and wooden lattice-work, painted green (see page 57). The roofs are all flat, and at twilight veiled figures may be seen outlined against the sunset sky.

Many of the interiors are beautiful. Once inside these buildings, one is astonished by the graceful courtyard and marble columns (see page 37). In localities where there is water flowing fountains are often seen, and palm and banana trees. Frequently tame gazelles come up and gaze at you. The courtyard is open to the sky and a great balcony runs around the second floor, opening into the women's apartment (see page 68).

Arab ladies are fond of visiting each other and may frequently be seen driving in their carriages from house to house, with thin black veils over their faces, through which one can see their profiles (compare page 54). The wives of some

### THE LIFE OF A PALM

"A palm begins to bear a few dates between the age of ten and twelve years. At fifteen it bears a good crop, and at thirty it is considered to be in its perfection. At forty it is still strong and vigorous. At the age of fifty the palm has grown so tall that it is weakened and its annual crop of dates is not abundant" (see text, page 117).

Photo by Lehnert and Landrock

### THE WAY DATES ARE GATHERED

The harvest is gathered in November and December and all the population of the oasis take part. A small boy, with a primitive sickle, climbs the palm; others follow him. The top boy cuts the great bunches and hands them to the boy beneath him, who passes them down from boy to boy until they reach the ground.

PICKING THE DATES  Photo by Lehnert and Landrock

When the clusters have been collected, busy workers begin to strip off the dates and gather them into heaps, roughly in accordance with their size and quality.

PACKING DATES FOR SHIPMENT  Photo by Lehnert and Landrock

When the dates have been sorted into the various grades, the best quality is then packed into wooden boxes of various sizes, containing from 22 to 66 pounds, loaded upon small donkeys, and taken to the adjacent village, to be transported later in large shipments to the nearest seaport.

Photo by Lehnert and Landrock

## CUTTING LEAVES BEFORE MAKING PALM WINE

"When no longer of use for bearing dates, most of the palm leaves are cut off and an incision is made in the top of the trunk just below where the leaves grow. A large pottery jar is hung underneath the incision and a bamboo tap fastened to carry the sap to the jar. This juice is called *lagmi* by the natives and is greatly esteemed as a beverage" (see text, page 117).

of the richer people are cultivated and charming, speaking several languages and quite in touch with the modern ideas of our Western world.

Until Khartum came under the British flag, Tripoli was one of the centers to which caravans came from the Sudan or the Sahara, bringing slaves, ivory, and ostrich feathers. Now the best qualities of feathers are sent direct to London by parcel post via Khartum, and it is no longer one of the centers for buying ostrich plumes, though second and third rate feathers can still be bought at Tripoli.

A thriving trade is done in esparto grass, which is shipped to England to be made into paper. The Japanese, by the way, are endeavoring to cultivate esparto grass in their country, and for the past two years they have imported quantities of this paper for their own use.

### THE GREAT WEEKLY MARKET

Every Tuesday morning a curious market formerly took place on the crescent-shaped beach, to which natives came from far and near to sell, barter, and exchange camels, donkeys, mules and horses, wool and hides, cereals, fruit, vegetables, and meat.

The market was a conglomeration of different tribes of northern Africa. Each tribe has its individual tattoo marks, or brands, some of which disfigure their faces terribly. Here the Bedouin from the Sahara has his head shaved and shampooed. Touaregs come in on their racing camels, called *mehara*, for supplies. They dislike towns and prefer their desert homes. The men are fierce and warlike, and can be distinguished from the other tribes by a cloth that almost covers their faces to protect them from the

cutting sandstorms. They usually wear thick woolen *bernouses*, and their heads are wound with a heavy, long turban or cloth. They claim that the sun burns through the garments, and in order to keep out the heat and sun they wear heavy clothes. even in midsummer.

Men from Timbuktu were always present at the market. dressed in the skins of wild animals and decorated with shells and animals' teeth. They wore face masks of skins and skulls, and danced to the beating of iron castanets, about two feet long, with heads as large as saucers. These men of Timbuktu remind one of the Indian medicine men of New Mexico and the Southwest.

Owing to the failure of crops during the past five years, thousands of Bedouins have come up from the interior of the Sahara, hoping to find work and a little food with which to sustain life. Poverty is so great that, until the Turkish-Italian war, one could see daily numbers of Bedouins, with small brooms made of palm leaves, sweeping up manure in the streets in the hope of finding a few undigested grains of barley or millet that they could eat.

V

## THE OASES OF NORTHERN AFRICA AND THE SAHARA

### ARAB SALUTATIONS

When, traveling in the interior of North Africa, one encounters a caravan or a band of mounted Bedouins, the salutation, *Salam aalikoum*, "Peace be upon you," may mean nothing to a stranger, *but how eagerly listened to* by one who knows, as it means his personal safety and the welfare of all that are with him.

Photo by Lehnert and Landrock

THE SOURCE OF LIFE OF THE OASES

"Many oases of northern Africa and the Sahara owe their existence to large springs of hot or cold water that bubble up close to each other, forming a great pool or natural reservoir, whence runs the stream that irrigates the oasis" (see text, page 99).

UNDER THE FURNACE OF HEAVEN

Photo by Bougault

The prime necessities in the cultivation of the palm are water and a hot sun. There is an old Arab proverb which, speaking of the palm, says "its feet shall be in a stream of water and its head in the furnace of heaven."

No one using the greeting *Salam aalikoum* would ever dare bring down the wrath of God upon his head by attempting to rob your caravan or murder you in your sleep. One can safely pitch one's tents next to the Bedouin using the above greeting, knowing that all will be well.

But if they do not salute you with those words, *then beware*. Danger lurks very near. The greeting *Salam aalikoum* is only used between Mohammedans. Should a Christian be in the caravan, they would say "May peace be upon those that accompany the stranger."

Even in speaking to a friend, or a stranger that one meets alone, one should always say "Peace be upon you"; *you*, used in the plural, because this man that you see alone is accompanied by the guardian angel, that you do not see, and you must salute them both.

No matter the state of one's birth, or power, or dignity, he that is on horseback should greet the man on foot. He that is walking should greet the man that he sees sitting down. A man on horseback should speak first to the man he meets riding a mule. A man on a mule should greet first a poor man riding a donkey.

The greeting should always be from the highest to the lowest, and never from the lowest to the highest. These rules of etiquette are most scrupulously kept, on account of the spirit of humility.

Should two men of equal rank pass each other, either on foot or horseback, then the younger man should first salute the elder man, in order to show respect to age.

Before eating there is a sort of grace asked that runs about like this: "O my God! Bless this that thou givest us to eat and drink, and when it has been consumed, reproduce it." *Always eat and drink* with the *right hand*, as only a demon eats and drinks with his left hand. After having finished drinking, one should say to the person: *Sahha*, "May Allah give you force!" He then replies, *Sel-meck!*

Photo by Lehnert and Landrock

## THE WATERFALL IN AN OASIS NEAR GABES

This waterfall only runs when the irrigation canals are full, for water in the desert is too precious to waste. Note the little Arab boy in the foreground, who, like all boys the world over, delights to play about in the water.

Photo by Lehnert and Landrock

THE LUNCH HOUR IN THE OASIS

"The Sheik's sons wait on their father, for nowhere in the world is such respect shown to a parent. A son may not smoke in the presence of his father. . . . In extreme southern Tunisia the more noise one makes in drinking tea, the better pleased appears the host" (see text, page 98).

Photo by Lehnert and Landrock

THE OLD WELL

The most dreaded scourge in Algeria and Tunisia is the locust. "It seems incredible that a thing so small and insignificant is so difficult to destroy. Build great fires and the swarms of crawling, wriggling nymphs will smother them, those in front being burned by millions, and those in the rear pushing on and passing over the burned bodies of the leaders. They will block and fill up a sluggish African stream, and the millions in the rear will pass over unharmed" (see text, page 78).

A RIVER BED NEAR AN OASIS                    Photo by Lehnert and Landrock

The rainy season generally begins in January and lasts two months, during which the temperature drops down to a mean of about 60 degrees. The summer lasts from May to October and is entirely rainless. During the autumn months occasional showers herald the approach of the rainy season proper.

## HOW THE ARABS DRINK TEA

Tea-making is a great ceremonial among the Arabs. It was first introduced in Morocco, and during the past 20 years has spread over all northern Africa; even the Puritan *Sennoussi* drink tea, coffee being forbidden.

Green tea is preferred to all others. I have sent presents of the best quality of English (Ceylon) tea to Arab Sheiks and Caids, asking them to tell me frankly how they liked it in comparison to their green tea, and the answer always came back that it was most excellent, but they did not like the flavor as well as their green tea.

A Troglodyte Sheik when serving tea sits in his rock cave behind a low table about five inches high, on which are arranged several tea-pots, often brought from Mecca, made of cop-

Photo by Lehnert and Landrock

DRAWING WATER FROM A DEEP WELL

In some parts of Tunisia it is necessary to bore to a great depth before water is reached. Over these deep wells a primitive arrangement of pulleys is erected and oxen are used to draw the water, as shown in the picture.

per or brass, and damascined with Persian designs in silver. As many tiny cups as there are guests are placed on the tray.

The Sheik's sons wait on their father, for *nowhere in the world* is such respect shown to a parent. A son may not smoke in the presence of his father.

An entire sugar loaf has been brought in and placed with a hammer near the Sheik. The teapots having been filled with water, they are set on glowing coals, often of dried camel's dung, as charcoal and wood are almost unknown. When the water boils, the tea is added

and great lumps of sugar are broken off with the hammer and put into the teapots.

Then each cup is slowly filled and the Sheik sips a little to see if it tastes right; then all the cups are emptied into the teapots and shaken up and then poured out again. This process is continued for a long time until the tea is almost like a liquor; mint and other ingredients are often added, so that the beverage does not resemble tea.

In extreme southern Tunisia the more noise one makes in drinking tea the better pleased appears the host.

Photo by Lehnert and Landrock

THE CITY OF NEFTA, TUNISIA (SEE TEXT, PAGES 117-122)

This city, which is really a collection of villages, stands on the western bank of the great salt lake of southern Tunisia, known as the Shott-el-Djerid. Once inlets of the Mediterranean, these Shotts are today not really lakes at all, but smooth, sunken areas, covered with incrustations of gray salt. During the rainy season, however, they hold a little water, which soon disappears.

## OASES OF NORTHERN AFRICA AND THE SAHARA

Many oases of northern Africa and the Sahara owe their existence to large springs of hot or cold water that bubble up close to each other, forming a great pool or natural reservoir, whence runs the stream that irrigates the oasis. This stream, called by Arabs an *oued*, is divided and subdivided a great many times, so that as much land as possible can be irrigated. The sand of the Sahara is not like that of the seashore, for when irrigated it becomes as fer-

tile as virgin soil; hence the fortunate owner of a garden with water privileges in an oasis, is, as a rule, a wealthy man.

In the thirteenth century there lived at Tozeur the Arab historian Iman Ibn Chabbath, who planned and carried out the simple system of irrigation that one sees today when roaming through the oases. The river (*oued*) that runs from the springs was divided into three streams of equal volume; each of these three main streams was again subdivided into seven smaller streams of equal volume, so that the oasis of

Photo by Lehnert and Landrock

A DESERTED INN IN TOZEUR

This picture, taken in the courtyard of a deserted inn in extreme southern Tunisia, shows how the rider sits a *mehari* or racing camel, and guides it by the pressure of his toes upon its neck (compare text, page 70).

Photo by Lehnert and Landrock

A GARDEN ON THE DESERT'S EDGE, NEAR TOZEUR (SEE PAGE 122)

Tozeur was entirely irrigated by these 21 streams.

The Iman Ibn Chabbath died in the year 1282 A. D. and was buried at Bled-el-Hader. His system of irrigation was copied in many other oases where there was plenty of water and it worked well for centuries.

Complications have arisen since the thirteenth century, and the ownership of water rights in an oasis today has become very tangled, so that the owners of the gardens in the oasis of Tozeur do not themselves know the exact amount of water they are entitled to, but leave it in the hands of their *khammes*, sort of head gardeners and experts on the volume of water the gardens of their masters are entitled to.

Centuries ago the owner of each garden had a right to let the water from one of the 21 equal streams flow (irrigate) over his ground for a fixed period of time every month during the year, so many days or so many nights, as the case might be. Time went on, and the heads of the families died. Three or four sons inherited the property and the garden would be divided into smaller parts.

An Arab being badly in need of funds and having more water than he actually needed for his garden would sell for a fixed sum the extra water that he did not use.

THE GREAT PRAYER AT BISKRA (I)

Photo by Bougault

Twice in the year a great prayer meeting is held on the plain outside the city of Biskra, in Algeria, which is attended by hundreds of devout Moslem men. This picture shows the first posture of prayer, that of standing.

THE GREAT PRAYER AT BISKRA (II)

Photo by Bougault

This picture shows the second posture of prayer, a profound inclination with the hands resting on the knees. The third posture is a complete prostration, as shown in the picture on page 103. The spectacle of these hundreds of men all bowing and chanting in unison is singularly impressive.

Photo by Bougault

THE GREAT PRAYER AT BISKRA (III)

The third posture of prayer is a complete prostration—the symbol of the adoration of the unity of God, the central doctrine of Islam. "The French government has allowed the natives absolute independence of thought and religion. In the far-off Troglodyte towns, where no mosques existed, some have been built by the government. This has been a very wise move, because it has endeared the French to the hearts of the Tunisians" (see text, page 61).

Photo by Bougault

THE GREAT PRAYER AT BISKRA (IV)

After the set liturgical prayers have been finished, the worshipers gather in a circle round an old Iman (or leader), who preaches to them. The sermon is not long, in deference to one of the Prophet's pithiest sayings, "The length of a man's prayers and the shortness of his sermons are signs of his common sense."

A BURIAL ON THE SAHARA      Photo by Lehnert and Landrock

The mourners are separated into two groups—one composed of men and the other of women—who are all howling and wailing at the top of their voices, the inevitable sign of mourning in the Orient.

The water rights became so complicated that the long periods of a night or a day were reduced to periods timed between the calls to prayer of the *muezzins.*

These were again shortened to a period equal to five minutes.

### HOW THE PERIODS OF TIME ARE MEASURED

Instead of an hour-glass the head gardener uses a primitive native pottery bowl, or in certain oases a gourd, with a tiny hole at the base. This implement takes just five minutes by the clock to empty itself of water. By means of a simple water gate one of the 21 equal streams is entirely turned into the garden to be irrigated.

The *khammes* plunges his gourd into the stream, fills it to the brim, and hangs it up and ties a knot into a long fiber of palm leaf to keep count of the number of periods. As soon as the gourd is empty the *khammes* refills it and ties a second knot.

He keeps this up until his number of periods have come to an end. The water gate is closed, the gourd wiped, and the small hole at the base carefully plugged to prevent sand and dirt from clogging the aperture.

Photo by Lehnert and Landrock

A North African graveyard is often much neglected; indeed, one Moslem sect thinks it meritorious to neglect their graves, believing it to be in accordance with the wishes of the Prophet. Graves are usually mounds of mud, with unbaked bricks set at the head.

A DISTANT VIEW OF EL-OUED       Photo by Lehnert and Landrock

Far out in the Sahara, in the extreme south of Tunisia, lies the almost unknown city of El-Oued, which is built upon a number of tiny oases which lie surrounded by the barren sands of the desert. Note the small group of mud houses on the right and the larger group of houses in the distant center.

Photo by Bougault

A GENERAL VIEW OF EL-OUED: NOTE THE SAND-DUNES SURROUNDING THE TOWN
(SEE PAGE 109)

A SMALL OASIS NEAR EL-OUED

Photo by Lehnert and Landrock

"The natives, centuries ago, dug enormous holes in the sand and planted palm groves in the holes, which were so deep that the roots of the palms have sufficient moisture throughout the year. A continual war is waged by the inhabitants against nature, for each sandstorm, and these are many, tends to fill in the holes and all the sand that is blown in has to be taken out again in small baskets" (see text, page 117, and pictures, pages 106 and 101).

Photo by Lehnert and Landrock

CHECKING THE MOVING SAND-DUNES

By planting certain coarse grasses along the ridges at the top of the sand-dunes, the desert Arabs are enabled to check to some extent the movement of the sand toward their date gardens.

Four hundred and seventy-nine *khammes* are employed in the oasis of Tozeur. The occupation descends as a rule from father to son and the men are greatly respected. At Tozeur the volume of water used during the period it takes a gourd to empty itself (five minutes) is equal to ten cubic meters* (2,641 gallons)

*1 liter contains 2.113 American pints, or 1.76 English pints.

1 cubic meter contains 264.18 American gallons of 231 cubic inches.

1 meter is equal to 39.37 inches.

1 kilogram is equal to 2⅕ pounds avoirdupois.

and such a water right is bought and sold in perpetuity for 120 to 180 francs.

The volume of water varies at each oasis. The combined springs at Tozeur have an output of 740 liters a second, or 44 cubic meters a minute and 63,936 cubic meters every 24 hours, which is equal to 16,879,104 gallons. The oasis of Nefta has a total output of over 800 liters a second.

Of course, these two oases are especially favored by nature; curiously enough, the more abundant the water the less the natives use it for performing their ablutions. Never have we seen such filthy natives as at Tozeur and Nefta. They use sand instead of water.

Between Nefta, Tunisia, and Biskra, in Algeria, in a region called Souf, there are to be found curious oases.

The most important is called El-Oued; it is a large and wealthy native town, and there is a French military outpost. The natives centuries ago dug enormous holes in the sand and planted palm groves in the holes, which were so deep that the roots of the palms have sufficient moisture throughout the year. A continual war is waged by the inhabitants of El-Oued against nature, for each sandstorm, and these are many, tends to fill in the holes, and all the sand that is blown in has to be taken out again in small baskets (see pages 101 and 107).

Most of us think of an oasis as an ideal cluster of tall palm trees with a beautiful pool, in which is reflected the azure sky and the waving palm leaves. Time and again while riding over the borders of the Sahara we have looked up and seen such an oasis with a wonderfully limpid lake, but it was a magic oasis that vanished on our approach, and the blue lake turned into scorching yellow sand—an optical illusion, a mirage!

MARKET DAY AT EL-OUED

Photo by Lehnert and Landrock

To the market at El-Oued come the inhabitants of those small but numerous oases which lie around this remote and little known city of the desert, and which are the only source of its trade.

THE WAVES OF THE DESERT                    Photo by Lehnert and Landrock

There is a greater similarity than would at first sight be supposed between the landscape of the desert and that of the ocean. The sand-dunes look like great petrified ocean breakers, broken here and there by little waves, caused by the action of wind.

Photo by Lehnert and Landrock

FOOTPRINTS IN THE SANDS OF TIME

Of late years many a man—and woman, too—has heard the "call of the desert," and, weary of the stress of life in our crowded, overcivilized communities, has gone out to seek the silent charm of those huge wastes and has come back invigorated in body and restored in mind.

Oases vary in size and are measured by the number of date palms in them; a small one contains several hundred palm trees and a large one 300,000 or 400,000.

### A LEGEND OF THE DATE PALM

The Arabs call the palm tree "My Aunt," and say that it resembles a human being more than any other variety of tree.

"Cut off its head and the palm will die. Its head likes sunshine and its feet (roots) like moisture."

An old Arab legend runs something like this: "When Allah created Adam, a few grains of dust fell between his fingers; these grains made the palm trees."

Another legend† runs as follows: "The Emperor of Byzantium wrote one day to the Caliph Amor Ben El Khattab: 'It has been told

†Translated from the Arabic Commentaries of Iman Ibn Amor Ibn Chabbath by Monsieur Lucien Fleury, who has kindly permitted the writer to use his unpublished work.

THE CREST OF THE WAVE                    Photo by Lehnert and Landrock

The charm of the desert landscape is the wonderful play of lights on dunes and hills of sand as they stretch away into the distance till sand joins sky. The insignificance of the camel in the center of the picture shows how high are the sand hills beyond.

me that in your country there grows a tree that bears pods, the shape of which reminds one of donkey's ears; when these open they expose to view a substance of immaculate whiteness, as white as milk, which afterward becomes the green color of an emerald, then turns as yellow as gold, to redden at last like a great ruby. This fruit is said to have the sweetness of taste of cake made of honey and butter and can be dried and used as food by the inhabitants of towns or by travelers on their journeys. If this report is true, surely this is a tree from Paradise!'"

Caliph Amor Ben El Khattab wrote back:

"That which has been told you is true, O King. Allah commanded Meriem beut Omran (the Virgin Mary) to take shelter under this tree when Aissa (Christ) was born. Believe, therefore, in Allah and do not acknowledge any other divinity!

A SCHOOL IN THE DESERT

"God said to Meriem beut Omran (the Virgin Mary), 'Go to the base of a palm tree and thou shalt give birth to a tender child, and nourish yourself with the fresh dates.'

"If God had known any better food, he certainly would have given them to Meriem when Christ was born.

"Allah reserved for the city of Medina the glory of being the refuge and dwelling place of The Prophet from the time of the *Hegira* throughout his life, and after his death the resting place of his blessed body, and has honor and glory as the Cradle of Islamism, for Medina is remarkable on account of its palm trees."

## THE DATE CROP
## AND HOW IT IS HARVESTED

The dates are gathered during the months of November and December, and this is the busiest time of the year. It seems as if all the male population, from feeble, gray-bearded old men to tiny infants, were gathered together in the oasis and divided into companies in the various great gardens.

A small boy with a primitive sickle climbs the date palm; others follow him. Before the first cluster of dates is cut every one on the tree and in the garden join in chanting a song of

A DESERT LANDSCAPE

Photo by Lehnert and Landrock

Those who know the nomad Arabs say that they are possessed of a love for the desert which is passionate and unquenchable. They love that perfect solitude, and in spite of all the hardships and danger of desert life, no reward is great enough to make them forsake it. Note the tracks made by the soft, spreading foot of the camel.

Photo by Lehnert and Landrock

ONE SOURCE OF FOOD AND WATER

"Living or dead, a camel is wealth to its master. To the Arabs of the Sahara a camel is like a reindeer to the Laplanders. Living, it carries the tents and provisions. It fears neither hunger, thirst, nor heat; its hair makes their tents (*gourbis*) and *bernouses*; the milk of the female nourishes the rich and the poor, enriches the dates, and fattens the horses" (see text, page 71).

thanks to Allah for having given them the harvest.

Then the top boy, deftly balancing himself between the palm leaves, quickly cuts the great bunches of transparent golden dates and hands them down one at a time to the boy under him, who passes them on to the youth below, and so on until they reach the ground (see page 88).

Then two clusters are carried at a time to a group of natives squatting on the ground, busily employed assorting the dates into different grades (see page 89). The best quality is then packed into wooden boxes of 10, 20, and 30 kilograms each (one kilogram equals two and one-fifth pounds) (see page 89), loaded upon small donkeys and taken to an adjacent village. When there are sufficient boxes ready to form a caravan, they are laden upon camels and taken to the nearest seaport or railroad station.

Before the boys descend from the palm tree that has just been denuded of its fruit a second

IN THE TRACKS OF A CARAVAN          Photo by Lehnert and Landrock

All that is left of a camel 24 hours after its death. When a camel is slaughtered on the march, the water in its stomach, its blood, and as much of its meat as possible is consumed by the members of the party. What is left falls to the share of the birds of prey, which appear in hundreds as, if by magic, out of a clear sky.

invocation is chanted, the signification of which runs as follows: "May Allah in his loving kindness preserve this palm tree from all harm and permit it to bear a good harvest in the season that is to come."

## HUNTING THE RATS

While the palms are being stripped of their fruit rat after rat is spied by the boys, who immediately climb after them. The rat takes refuge on the end of a palm leaf, while scores of infants too young to climb gather underneath.

The older boys who have climbed the tree shake the leaves until the rat jumps or falls off. In spite of the height, the rat never seems to be hurt.

There is a wild scrimmage among the small children to catch it, and one of them carries it in triumph to an Arab, who immediately cuts off the rat's teeth and fastens a string made of palm fiber to its hind leg. It is then given to one of the tiny girls or boys as a plaything.

About three o'clock of an afternoon, when the day's work is almost finished and many palms have been stripped of their fruit, there is

Photo by Lehnert and Landrock

DESERT SCOUTING: A NOMAD ON HIS MEHARI

"In the interior of northern Africa is a superb race of camels, known as the *mehara* (singular, *mehari*), or racing camels. . . . Ancient writers speak of camels used by the army of Xerxes, more than 2,000 years ago, that had the speed of the fastest horses; these were doubtless *mehara*" (see text, page 66).

not an infant to be seen without at least one rat, frequently two or three. They are fat and have soft, silver-gray skins, with white bellies. These unfortunate playthings are finally killed, split open, broiled over coals, and eaten.

## THE LIFE OF THE PALM

A palm begins to bear a few dates between the age of 10 and 12 years. At 15 it bears a good crop and at 30 it is considered in its perfection; at 40 it is still strong and vigorous, but no longer gives forth shoots. At the age of 50 the palm has grown so tall that it is weakened and its annual crop of dates is not so abundant.

When no longer of use for bearing dates most of the palm leaves are cut off and an incision is made in the top of the trunk just below where the leaves grow. A large pottery jar is hung underneath the incision and a bamboo tap fastened to carry the sap to the jar.

This juice is called *lagmi* by the natives and is greatly esteemed as a beverage. It is bluish white in color and has an insipid sweetish taste when fresh, rather refreshing when one is

Photo by Lehnert and Landrock

AT THE CLOSE OF DAY: A MEHARI AND HIS OWNERS AT REST

"*Mehara* (racing camels) are usually fawn-colored, with soft, intelligent eyes. They have pointed ears like gazelles. Their chests are very well developed, and they have a small girth almost like that of a greyhound. Their
slender legs bulge with muscles as hard as steel" (see text, pages 71-72).

thirsty. It ferments quickly and is then extremely
intoxicating. Europeans do not like it.

Every date-bearing palm tree over 20 years
old is taxed by the Tunisian government.

The average yearly harvest of common
dates amounts to 32,000 quintals of 100 kilograms, or 7,040,000 pounds, and the *Degla* variety 4,000 quintals of 100 kilograms, or 880,000
pounds. When one realizes that the above figures are for one oasis, and that within 15 miles
of Tozeur are two other great oases—Nefta and
Deggache, often called El-Oudiane—that yield

an equal amount of dates, one begins to com-
prehend the importance of the date harvest.

Only the female palm bears dates. The
male palm has a few large white flowers that
somewhat resemble ostrich plumes. Unless fertilized artificially the female palm produces few,
if any, dates. A small piece of the male flower
about the size of an ear of wheat is tied into the
pod of the female flower. Any flower not thoroughly fertilized produces half of the bunch of
dates immature and hard, useless as food, and
despised even by camels.

THE SAVIOUR OF THREE

Photo by Lehnert and Landrock

"A *mehari* (racing camel) on the war-path can save three men. Two ride him and the third takes hold of its tail and is pulled along. The latter changes places with the riders at intervals. When a war party has lost so many camels that there remain but one camel for three men, it always retreats" (see text, page 71).

A CARAVAN ON THE MARCH     Photo by Lehnert and Landrock

## SCIENTIFIC AGRICULTURE WOULD VASTLY INCREASE THE DATE

On visiting the plantation of a French friend I noticed that all of his date palms bore perfect clusters of well-ripened dates, and expressed my astonishment that his were so perfect when the adjoining gardens owned by Arabs had only one-half or one-third of their dates ripened, the remainder being a total loss.

He laughed and said, "You know that it is the custom of the country to pay the men partly in dates. I told all of my Arab gardeners that if they neglected properly to fertilize the female palm trees that their pay would be in the immature, useless dates. Since then there has been no shirking of the fertilization and my date harvest has increased enormously; before it was too

much trouble for the Arabs to climb up and attend thoroughly to each palm and they frequently slighted their work."

This gentleman is an up-to-date "colonial," born in Tunisia of French parents. He is one of the rare exceptions, a Frenchman that owns property in an oasis, and it is interesting to compare the result of his agricultural methods and those of the Arabs.

He has been in America and studied our methods and has adopted what he found best suited to his work in southern Tunisia, and he attributes a great part of his success to the Department of Agriculture at Washington, D. C.

He has a trial garden where one-half is planted by the old Arab method, the other half according to the latest American and French agricultural methods. He also uses chemical fer-

Photo by Lehnert and Landrock

## THE NEVER-ENDING STRIFE OF SAND AND WIND

The action of the wind builds up huge and ever-shifting hills of desert sand. One can judge of their great size by comparing the sitting figures at the foot of the hill with the man and his camel at the top.

tilizers, for this particular garden has been cultivated since the Roman occupation and the ground probably has never been fertilized.

The result of his work appears like magic. Palm trees planted four years ago and fertilized have grown as large as Arab palm trees ten years old. Everything seems to thrive, and one sees underneath the superb date palms, orange and lemon trees, figs, pomegranates, apricots, and bananas and grapevines and numerous varieties of vegetables.

Were the gardens of the oases owned by Europeans and cultivated with modern methods the result would be phenomenal. Unfortunately the Arab owners of the oases are not fond of hard work and content themselves with comparatively little.

The beautiful oases of southern Tunisia are as near an approach to the Garden of Eden as one can hope to find. Almost everything thrives that can be grown in a semi-tropical country, owing to the rich soil and abundance of water.

To give a vague idea of an oasis, let me describe that of Tozeur, in southern Tunisia. Eleven thousand Arabs live underneath the shadow of the palms of this oasis, which covers an area of about 2,200 acres (900 hectares), and 4,000 occupy small villages on the outskirts. Most of them were born and have always lived in this oasis, and when they die they will be buried in the desert sand near Tozeur.

The oasis has nourished these 15,000 souls and many thousands more; their wants and needs are simple. Families composed of husband and wife, or wives, and three or four children frequently live on less than ten cents (50 centimes) a day.

Their mainstay consists of dried dates and a few boiled beans with a little pure olive oil.

At almost any turn of the road in the oasis one can buy from an Arab vender, crouched over a large Standard Oil can and fanning the live coals, a copious supply of beans cooked until they are mealy and ladled out of the can boiling (see page 95). One cent buys enough for a very hungry man.

### THE GREAT DATE MARKETS

Caravans of nomads come from far and near to buy the dates.

An hour before sunset the sand dunes around Tozeur seem to be alive with camels, and caravan after caravan arrives and encamps for the night just outside the town. A curious acrid odor pervades the air, coming from the thousands of camels. The noise is deafening; each camel snarls and groans when forced to kneel; baby camels bleat like a calf, and swarthy men of the desert call to each other in shrill voices.

There are camels of all ages and sizes, dark brown, fawn, and cream colored. Frequently six or eight large male camels stampede and, rushing to another camp, become mixed up with two or three hundred camels of another caravan.

The burdens and saddles are placed in a large circle that forms a sort of wall, and the camels are forced to kneel inside in rows close to each other. When once down, their knees are tied so that they cannot escape during the night. It is no small matter to settle a caravan composed of four hundred camels.

At last, when the camels are all secured, small camp-fires are built of dried sage-brush and a frugal meal of beans is cooked and some dried dates eaten afterward. The wants of these nomads are few; they are like happy, primitive children.

As the twilight fades into a wonderful deep blue and the camp-fires flicker and die down a great silence falls over the oasis; the barking of the dogs has ceased; the camels are asleep.

Only the motionless figures of a few nomads guarding their caravans wrap their *bernouses* more tightly about them as they stand outlined against a blue-black sky, for the cold is bitter. The sleeping men, wearied from their long march, lie huddled close together, as near as possible to the camels for warmth and protection from the wind.

Suddenly the piercing cry of a *muezzin* breaks the stillness of the African night, and it is taken up by a score of other *muezzins* in their fifth and last call to prayer of the day, and Bedouins dwelling in their tents made of woven camel's or goat's hair far out on the sand dunes distinctly hear the words "Allah is Allah! there is no God but Allah! Mohammed is his Prophet!"

# FURTHER READING

Albert Hourani, *A History of the Arab Peoples* (1991) is a panoramic view of Arab history and culture. *The Shaping of the Arabs* by Joel Carmichael (1967) is a general historical survey which includes an interpretation of the Maghreb. See also Jamil M. Abun-Nasr, *A History of the Mahgreb* (1971); Ronald Steel, ed. *North Africa* (1967); Jacques Berque, *French North Africa* (1962); and Jane Soames Nickerson, *A Short History of North Africa* (1968).

# INDEX

# CONTRIBUTORS

General Editor FRED L. ISRAEL is an award-winning historian. He received the Scribe's Award from the American Bar Association for his work on the Chelsea House series *The Justices of the United States Supreme Court*. A specialist in American history, he was general editor for Chelsea's *1897 Sears Roebuck Catalog*. Dr. Israel has also worked in association with Arthur M. Schlesinger, jr. on many projects, including *The History of the U.S. Presidential Elections* and *The History of U.S. Political Parties*. He is senior consulting editor on the Chelsea House series *Looking into the Past: People, Places, and Customs*, which examines past traditions, customs, and cultures of various nations.

Senior Consulting Editor ARTHUR M. SCHLESINGER, JR. is the pre-eminent American historian of our time. He won the Pulitzer Prize for his book *The Age of Jackson* (1945), and again for *A Thousand Days* (1965). This chronicle of the Kennedy Administration also won a National Book Award. He has written many other books, including a multi-volume series, *The Age of Roosevelt*. Professor Schlesinger is the Albert Schweitzer Professor of the Humanities at the City University of New York, and has been involved in several other Chelsea House projects, including the *American Statesmen* series of biographies on the most prominent figures of early American history.